Best Easy Day Hikes
San Diego

Help Us Keep This Guide Up to Date

Every effort has been made by the author and editors to make this guide as accurate and useful as possible. However, many things can change after a guide is published—trails are rerouted, regulations change, facilities come under new management, etc.

We would love to hear from you concerning your experiences with this guide and how you feel it could be improved and kept up to date. While we may not be able to respond to all comments and suggestions, we'll take them to heart and we'll also make certain to share them with the authors. Please send your comments and suggestions to the following address:

The Globe Pequot Press
Reader Response/Editorial Department
P.O. Box 480
Guilford, CT 06437

Or you may e-mail us at:

editorial@GlobePequot.com

Thanks for your input, and happy trails!

Best Easy Day Hikes Series

Best Easy Day Hikes
San Diego

Second Edition

Sean O'Brien

Updated by Allen Riedel

FALCONGUIDES ®

GUILFORD, CONNECTICUT
HELENA, MONTANA

AN IMPRINT OF ROWMAN & LITTLEFIELD

FALCONGUIDES®

Copyright © 2009 by Rowman & Littlefield

Falcon, FalconGuides, and Outfit Your Mind are registered trademarks of Rowman & Littlefield.

TOPO! Explorer software and SuperQuad source maps courtesy of National Geographic Maps. For information about TOPO! Explorer, TOPO!, and Nat Geo Maps products, go to www.topo.com or www .natgeomaps.com

Project editor: Jessica Haberman
Layout artist: Kevin Mak
Maps: Ryan Mitchell © Rowman & Littlefield

Library of Congress Cataloging-in-Publication Data.

Riedel, Allen
  Best easy day, hikes San Diego / Allen Riedel. – 2nd ed.
      p. cm. – (Falconguides)
  ISBN 978-0-7627-5113-6
  1. Hiking–California–San Diego County–Guidebooks. 2. San Diego County (Calif.)–Guidebooks. I. Title.
  GV199.42.C22S265 2009
  796.5109794'98–dc22

                                                    2009007040

Printed in the United States of America

Distributed by NATIONAL BOOK NETWORK

Contents

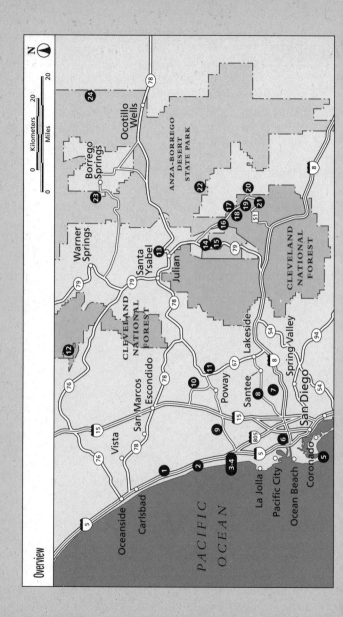

Overview

Desert Hikes

Map Legend

═══⟨15⟩═══	Interstate Highway
══⟨101⟩══	U.S. Highway
══⟨78⟩══	State Highway
══⟨51⟩══	Local/Forest Road
= = = =	Unimproved Road
- - - - - - -	Trail
▬▬▬▬▬	Featured Route
⊢—⊢—⊢	Railroad Grade
〰	River/Creek
⋯⟋	Intermittent Stream
— ⋯	Marsh/Swamp
▭	State Forest/Park/Preserve
▭	National Forest/Monument
▲	Campground
❓	Information
🛉	Lighthouse
🅿	Parking
▲	Peak
🛆	Picnic Area
■	Point of Interest
⚲	Spring
○	Town
❻	Trailhead
≋	Waterfall
N ⬇	True North (Magnetic North is approximately 15.5° East)

Introduction

San Diego County seems to have it all: friendly locals, beaches as far as the eye can see, a lively downtown district, and a world-famous mild climate. It's no wonder city leaders have dubbed it "America's Finest City."

This bounty of opportunity holds true for the outdoor lover. There are literally hundreds of miles of trails within an hour's drive of downtown.

However, it is the diversity of the hikes found within the county, not just their quantity, that sets San Diego apart. Lagoons, majestic sandstone cliffs, and miles of sandy beaches line the coast and attract visitors from around the world.

Farther inland, many of the sinuous oak- and sycamore-lined canyon bottoms have been set aside as nature preserves. It's in these canyons that on quiet mornings deer, coyotes, and bobcats can sometimes be spotted browsing through the dew-wet grasses while the modern world races by on the mesa tops above.

To the east, coastal mountains form the gentle spine of the county, capturing winter rains and sheltering deep forests, year-round streams, and an abundance of wildlife. In these mountains, it's easy to imagine yourself hundreds of miles from civilization, while in reality you are only a short drive from the city center.

San Diego's climate echoes its topography, and each microclimate—coast, inland, mountains—possesses unique weather and temperature patterns. On the same day when winter snows may require chains for your car tires in the mountains, the hikes along the coast may be pleasant and dry. Likewise, as the summertime temperatures soar into the triple digits inland, the coasts and mountains are often 20 degrees cooler. The fact is, no matter what time of year, there is probably somewhere within San Diego County where the weather is perfect for hiking.

Inside this guide you'll find a selection of short, less-strenuous hikes that demand little more than a sturdy pair of shoes. The hikes are grouped geographically—especially in the mountains—in the belief that you'd rather be hiking than driving. Most are less than 5 miles long; all follow established trails and avoid most route-finding difficulties.

There is something here for everyone, including those looking for a workout. To approximate how long it will take you to complete a given trail, use the standard of 2 miles per hour, adding time if you are not a strong hiker or are traveling with small children, and subtracting time if you are in good shape. Add time for picnics, rest stops, or other activities you plan for your outing.

I've listed the pertinent U.S. Geological Survey 7.5-minute topographical map with each hike for your reference. Other maps can be found through the USDA Forest Service and at respective parks.

So, lace up your shoes, grab a water bottle, and come enjoy some of the natural wonders of San Diego!

Zero Impact

The trails that weave through San Diego's parklands are heavily used and sometimes take a real beating. Because of their proximity to pollution and dense population we—as trail users and advocates—must be especially vigilant to make sure our passing leaves no lasting mark. If we all left our mark on the landscape, the parks and wildlands eventually would be destroyed.

These trails can accommodate plenty of human travel if everybody treats them with respect. Just a few thoughtless, badly mannered, or uninformed visitors can ruin them for everyone who follows.

The Falcon Zero-Impact Principles

- Leave with everything you brought with you.
- Leave no sign of your visit.
- Leave the landscape as you found it.

Litter is the scourge of all trails. It is unsightly, polluting, and potentially dangerous to wildlife. Pack out all your own trash, including biodegradable items like orange peels. You should also pack out garbage left trailside by other hikers. Store a plastic bag in your pack to use for trash removal.

Don't approach or feed any wild creatures—the ground squirrel eyeing your snack food is best able to survive if it remains self-reliant, since it is not likely to find cookies along the trail when winter comes.

Never pick flowers or gather plants or insects. So many people visit these trails that the cumulative effect of individual impacts can be great.

Stay on established trails. Shortcutting and cutting switchbacks promote erosion. Select durable surfaces, like rocks, logs, or sandy areas, for resting spots. Be courteous by not making loud noises while hiking.

Some of the trails described in this guide also are used by horseback riders and mountain bikers. Acquaint yourself with proper trail etiquette and be courteous. Consider volunteering time to trail maintenance projects, giving something back to the parks and trails you enjoy.

If possible, use outhouses at trailheads or along the trail. If not, pack in a lightweight trowel and a plastic bag so that you can bury your waste 6 to 8 inches deep. Pack out used toilet paper in a plastic bag. Make sure you relieve yourself at least 300 feet away from any surface water or boggy spot, and off any established trail.

Remember to abide by the golden rule of backcountry travel: If you pack it in, pack it out! Keep your impact to a minimum by taking only pictures and leaving only footprints.

Practice zero impact principles—put your ear to the ground and listen carefully. Thousands of people coming behind you are thankful for your courtesy and good sense.

Play It Safe

Generally, hiking in San Diego is a safe and fun way to explore the outdoors. Though there are no guarantees, there is much you can do to help ensure each outing is a safe and enjoyable one. Below, you'll find an abbreviated list of hiking dos and don'ts, but by no means should this list be considered comprehensive. You are strongly encouraged to verse yourself in the art of backcountry travel.

Know the basics of first aid, including how to treat bleeding, bites and stings, and fractures, strains, or sprains. Few of the hikes are so remote that help can't be reached within a short time, but you'd be wise to carry and know how to use simple supplies, such as over-the-counter pain relievers, bandages, and ointments. Pack a first-aid kit on each excursion.

San Diego is renowned for its sunny skies and warm climate. While this can be a boon for year-round hiking, it nevertheless presents its own set of challenges. The sun can be unrelenting; carry a sunscreen with a minimum 15 SPF and apply it often. The weather also can change abruptly—especially in the winter and spring months (November through April). Carry a windbreaker and other clothing items to protect you from sudden and dramatic temperature changes and/or rain. Remember, summer thunderstorms aren't uncommon in San Diego's mountains and may bring dangers such as lightning, hail, and high winds.

The hills and mountains are home to a variety of wildlife, from squirrels to mountain lions. Squirrels can be host to disease, and mountain lions may attack if prompted by hunger. Rattlesnakes may be found on any of the hikes described, particularly from early spring to mid-fall. Watch where you put your hands and feet. If given a chance, most rattlesnakes will try to avoid a confrontation.

The same flora and fauna that make hiking such a relief from the daily grind also possess potential hazards for unwary hikers. Know how to identify poison oak, which can be plentiful in the canyons of San Diego.

Ticks are another pest to be avoided. They hang in the brush waiting to drop on warm-blooded animals (people included). Check for ticks and remove any before they have a chance to bite.

San Diego County is an arid region with frequent high temperatures—it is wise to bring more drinking water than you think you'll need. Generally, bring 32 ounces for each hour of hiking per person. Most free-flowing water should be considered unsafe to drink if untreated.

You'll enjoy each of these hikes—whether short and easy or long and strenuous—much more if you wear good socks and appropriate footwear.

Carry a comfortable day pack containing snacks and/or lunch, and extra clothing. Maps are not necessary, but they are fun to have along. You also can pack other items to increase your enjoyment of the hike, like a camera, a manual to help identify plants and wildflowers, and binoculars.

Coastal Hikes

The Pacific Ocean sits like a glimmering jewel to the west of San Diego. These hikes explore its immediate shoreline and the nearby habitats surrounding the beach.

As you make your way along the trail on the five hikes that follow, you'll travel through lagoons, down towering coastal sandstone bluffs, and discover what life was like in San Diego County more than one hundred years ago. Along the way you'll feast on a variety of spectacular vistas of the city, the mountains to the east, and the world-famous Pacific blue.

1 Batiquitos Lagoon

Take a lovely stroll along an ocean-side wetland interpretative trail with fantastic opportunities for bird-watching.

Distance: 2.8 miles out and back
Approximate hiking time: 1.5 hours
Elevation gain: 40 feet
Trail surface: Packed dirt
Best season: Year-round
Other trail users: Joggers, dogs, strollers, wheelchairs
Canine compatibility: Leashed dogs permitted
Fees and permits: None
Maps: USGS Encinitas, CA TOPO CD 10
Contact: Batiquitos Lagoon Foundation, P.O. Box 130491, Carlsbad, CA 92013; (760) 931-0800; www.batiquitosfoundation .org

Finding the trailhead: To reach Batiquitos Lagoon Ecological Reserve from the junction of Interstates 5 and 8, take I-5 north for 25.2 miles to Poinsettia Lane and turn right (east). Drive 0.3 mile to Batiquitos Drive and turn right (south). Drive 2 miles and turn right into the parking lot.

The Hike

Hemmed in by housing developments, a golf course, and one of the busiest freeways in the world, Batiquitos Lagoon won't be confused with the wilderness backcountry. However, if you're an avid bird-watcher (or would like to try this popular pastime), Batiquitos Lagoon provides excellent opportunities to view a number of endangered species.

Interpretive signs along the trail illustrate the more threatened birds found around the lagoon, as well as the rare and endangered species that visit. These include the

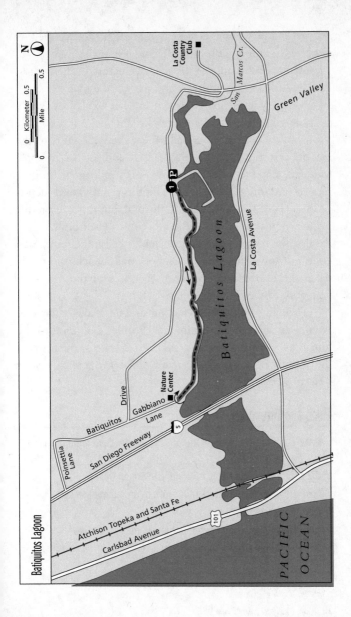

red-necked phalarope, elegant tern, marbled godwit, yellow warbler, California least tern, Belding savannah sparrow, and snowy plover. Because of the sensitive nature of these birds, read and follow the notices—and stay on the trail.

Even if you're not interested in watching birds, you'll find the wide, level trail a peaceful respite.

From the parking lot, walk down the wide stairs to the lagoon, turn right (west) onto the trail, and pass an interpretive sign. Enter a eucalyptus grove at 0.4 mile, and continue to a second interpretive sign. From this point, a bird identification book and binoculars are helpful, but the interpretive plaques point out some of the more threatened birds.

Pass the Aviara Golf Course clubhouse on the right, then continue down the wide and smooth trail, which runs parallel to the nearby links. Enter a second eucalyptus grove as you walk to the third interpretive sign.

Leave the golf course behind as you make your way around an inlet in the lagoon at 0.9 mile. Continue to the fourth and final interpretive sign at 1.2 miles, which sits at the mouth of a wooded canyon. To return, retrace your steps to your car.

Miles and Directions

0.0 From the east side of the parking lot, descend the dirt trail to the main trail.

0.1 Turn right and head west along the main trail.

0.4 Pass through a eucalyptus grove to an interpretive sign.

0.9 Pass a small inlet.

1.4 Reach the visitor center. Return via the same route.

2.8 Arrive back at the parking area.

2 San Elijo Lagoon

Stroll beside a lovely lagoon, take in hillside views, and bird-watch in an urban but tranquil setting.

Distance: 5 miles out and back
Approximate hiking time: 2.5 hours
Elevation gain: 100 feet
Trail surface: Packed dirt
Best season: Year-round, although heavy winter rains often submerge the first 0.25 mile of the trail, making it impassable.
Other trail users: Joggers, strollers, wheelchairs, dogs
Canine compatibility: Leashed dogs permitted
Fees and permits: None
Maps: USGS Encinitas, CA TOPO CD 10
Contact: San Elijo Lagoon Conservancy, P.O. Box 23064, Encinitas, CA 92023; (760) 436-3944; www.sanelijo.org

Finding the trailhead: To reach San Elijo Lagoon Ecological Preserve from the junction of Interstates 5 and 8, take I-5 north for 18.4 miles to Manchester Avenue. Turn left (east) onto Manchester Avenue and head 0.3 mile and park alongside the thoroughfare.

The Hike

Great blue herons stand still as statues in the rippling water. Snowy egrets perform Tai Chi–like movements as they forage for supper. Cattails wave in the wind and the setting sun casts a golden hue as far as the eye can see. Another day ends on San Elijo Lagoon.

According to interpretive signs found within this natural haven, only 10 percent of San Diego County's original coastal salt marsh remains. As you hug the shore of San Elijo

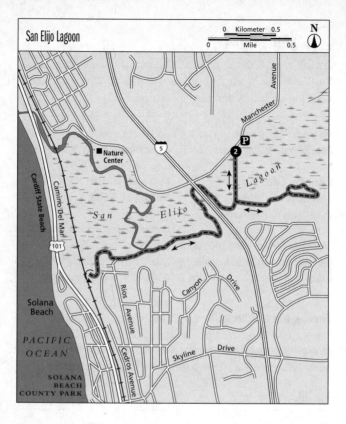

San Elijo Lagoon

0 Kilometer 0.5
0 Mile 0.5

N

Manchester Avenue

Nature Center

5

P 2

Lagoon

San Elijo

Cardiff State Beach

Camino Del Mar

101

Solana Beach

Rios Avenue

Canyon Drive

Cedros Avenue

Skyline Drive

PACIFIC OCEAN

SOLANA BEACH COUNTY PARK

Lagoon, you'll be glad that this particular parcel of water, sand, and sky has escaped development.

After an inauspicious beginning, with the din of the freeway in your ears, this hike becomes scenic and enjoyable. Like Batiquitos Lagoon to the north, San Elijo is an excellent location for identifying birds.

From your roadside parking, walk to the entrance and head south across the man-made causeway. Turn left at the trail junction at 0.3 mile, angling away from the noisy freeway. From here, the trail meanders alongside the lagoon and eventually reaches a hill and overlook. Enjoy the views and vantage and continue to the original trail junction. This time make two right turns, always heading for the freeway. Head under the freeway overpass on a narrow wooden bridge at 1.75 miles. Make a left (south) turn and follow the well-graded trail.

Leave the din of the freeway by traversing a hillside to the trail along the lagoon. Survey the views of the lagoon as you amble along the shore to an interpretive sign. Listen for the call of the threatened gnatcatcher (which sounds like a kitten) as you walk up into coastal sage scrub.

Make a right (north) turn at the gate on North Rios Avenue at 2.75 miles and head down the dirt road back into the preserve. Contour around to the western side of the lagoon, where a small trail leads up to tantalizing views of Seaside Reef and the Pacific Ocean. To get back to your car, retrace your steps through the wetlands.

Miles and Directions

0.0 Head south across the causeway.

0.3 Make a left turn and walk along the lagoon.

1.0 Reach a hill and overlook of the eastern side of the lagoon.

1.4 Continue straight at the trail junction. Make two right turns, always aiming for the freeway.

1.75 Pass under the freeway on a narrow wooden bridge.

2.75 Make a right turn at the North Rios Avenue gate and head down the dirt road back into the preserve.

3.0 Retrace your steps to the causeway.

4.6 Turn left and cross the causeway back to Manchester Avenue.

5.0 Arrive back at Manchester Avenue.

3 Guy Fleming Trail

Hike on the easiest trail in Torrey Pines State Natural Reserve; enjoy ocean views and spectacular scenery.

Distance: 0.65-mile lollipop
Approximate hiking time: 0.5 hour
Elevation gain: 50 feet
Trail surface: Packed dirt
Best season: Year-round
Other trail users: None
Canine compatibility: No dogs allowed

Fees and permits: Parking/day-use fee per vehicle
Maps: USGS Del Mar, CA TOPO CD 10
Contact: Torrey Pines State Natural Reserve and State Beach, 12600 North Torrey Pines Road, San Diego 92037; (858) 755-2063; www.parks.ca.gov/default.asp?page_id=657

Finding the trailhead: To reach Torrey Pines State Reserve from the junction of Interstates 5 and 8, take I-5 north for 12.6 miles to Carmel Valley Road and turn left (west). Drive 1.5 miles and turn left onto North Torrey Pines Road. The park entrance is 0.8 mile ahead on the right. Drive 0.5 mile on Torrey Pines Park Road and park after the first switchback on the road.

The Hike

Perched atop massive sandstone bluffs above a lonely stretch of coastline, one of the world's rarest trees, *Pinus torreyana,* or Torrey pine, has found a lasting and protected home. Once widespread along the Southern California coastline, these trees have been restricted by great changes in climate and landscape since the last ice age. Now they are found native in only two locations: in and around this reserve and on Santa Rosa Island near Santa Barbara.

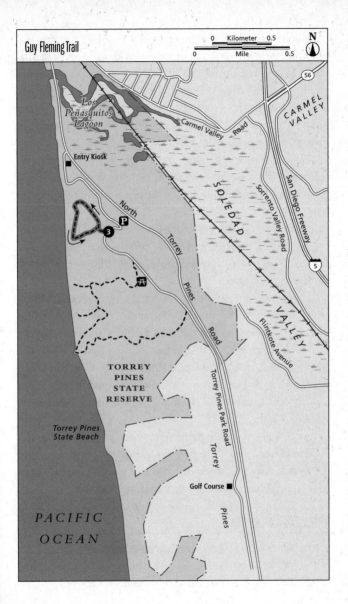

Guy Fleming Trail

0   Kilometer   0.5
0   Mile   0.5

N

56

Los
Peñasquitos
Lagoon

Carmel Valley   Road

CARMEL
VALLEY

Entry Kiosk

North

P

3

Torrey

Pines

SOLEDAD

Sorrento Valley Road

San Diego Freeway

5

Road

Flinkote Avenue

VALLEY

TORREY
PINES
STATE
RESERVE

Torrey Pines
State Beach

Torrey Pines Park Road

Torrey

PACIFIC

OCEAN

Golf Course

Pines

You'll have ample opportunity to enjoy these rare and beautiful trees as you stroll around this short loop, which is accessible to people with disabilities. The views from atop the sandstone bluffs overlooking the Pacific are awe-inspiring—especially at sunset. To truly appreciate the beauty of Torrey Pines State Reserve, spend some time savoring its unique stretch of coastline.

From the marked trailhead, amble down the smooth, relatively flat trail to a junction, where you'll turn right (north) and pass interesting sandstone formations on your left.

Stroll through the shade of a lovely stand of Torrey pines as you walk along the north side of a hillside. Glimpses of the Los Peñasquitos Lagoon and Torrey Pines State Beach complete the scene.

Leave the pines behind for sunny, spring-wildflower-covered hills. At 0.2 mile, a spectacular overlook provides incredible panoramas of the San Diego County coastline. On sunny days, reefs and kelp beds can be seen through the aquamarine water. Head south along the bluff top past cacti, wildflowers, and drought- and beetle-ravaged Torrey pines to a second overlook at the bottom of a set of railroad-tie stairs (0.3 mile).

After enjoying the panorama, turn your back on the coast and head inland, noting the game trails that run along the bottom of the canyon on your right. Complete the loop near the trailhead and continue back to your car.

Miles and Directions

0.0 From the parking area continue south to the signed trailhead.

0.1 Turn right and follow the loop counterclockwise.

0.2 Reach the first scenic overlook.

0.3 Pass the second scenic overlook.

0.6 Turn right to exit the loop.

0.65 Arrive back at the trailhead.

4 Razor Point/Beach Trail/Broken Hill Trail Loop

Distance: 3-mile loop

Approximate hiking time: 2 hours

Elevation gain: 400 feet

Trail surface: Packed dirt

Best season: Year-round, although heavy winter rains may make the trail impassable.

Other trail users: Joggers

Canine compatibility: No dogs allowed

Fees and permits: Parking/day-use fee per vehicle

Maps: USGS Del Mar, CA TOPO CD 10

Contact: Torrey Pines State Natural Reserve and State Beach, 12600 North Torrey Pines Road, San Diego 92037; (858) 755-2063; www.parks.ca.gov/default .asp?page_id=657

Finding the trailhead: To reach Torrey Pines State Reserve from the junction of Interstates 5 and 8, take I-5 north for 12.6 miles to Carmel Valley Road and turn left (west). Drive 1.5 miles and turn left onto North Torrey Pines Road. The park entrance is 0.8 mile ahead on the right. The best parking for the Beach Trail/Broken Hill Trail Loop is the visitor center parking lot 0.8 mile from the entrance.

The Hike

This hike will take you to the very brink of the Pacific, passing through scattered Torrey pines (one of Earth's rarest

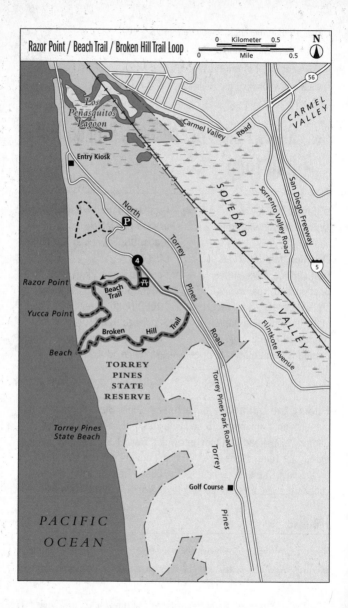

Razor Point / Beach Trail / Broken Hill Trail Loop

Kilometer
0   0.5
Mile
0   0.5

N

Los Peñasquitos Lagoon

Carmel Valley Road

CARMEL VALLEY

56

Entry Kiosk

North

P

SOLEDAD

Sorrento Valley Road

San Diego Freeway

I5

4

Razor Point

Beach Trail

Yucca Point

Broken Hill Trail

Beach

Torrey Pines Road

VALLEY

Flintkote Avenue

TORREY PINES STATE RESERVE

Torrey Pines State Beach

Torrey Pines Park Road

Torrey Pines

Golf Course

PACIFIC OCEAN

species of trees) and past two magnificent viewpoints on the 350-foot sandstone bluffs.

The trailhead is across the street from the visitor center near the restrooms. Follow the signs to Razor Point as you parallel the Canyon of the Swifts, noting the surreal and twisted forms of Torrey pines killed by a beetle infestation. Pause at Razor Point Lookout—with expansive views of the Pacific Coast and eroded sandstone bluffs—before retracing your steps for 200 yards back to the Beach Trail junction (0.6 mile). Turn right (west) and make a 0.25-mile detour to Yucca Point Overlook at 1.1 miles before returning to the main trail.

Head for the Pacific on Beach Trail, which winds its way down a shallow canyon to the coast. The beach at last! But not just any beach—the trail eventually leads to one of the most remote stretches of coastline in San Diego County. Use caution as you traverse the final ledge to the sand and breakers. An excellent picnic spot is just to the south. At high tide, the ocean can entirely swallow the sandy beach. However, lower tides make for very enjoyable walking, especially to the south. Be warned: Clothing-optional Black's Beach is 2 miles in that direction.

This path doesn't take you pass Black's, however. Instead, it leaves the beach and climbs Broken Hill (1.5 miles), which is covered with coastal sage and offers little shade. Tighten your shoelaces and catch your breath—it's a long climb to the top. Fortunately, the cool Pacific breezes should provide some relief as you climb to the top of the majestic, golden sandstone bluff.

As the climb begins to ease, turn left (north) at the junction of North Fork Trail at 2.5 miles, which provides for excellent views of Fern Canyon. At the junction with the paved road, make a left (north) turn, and head back to the visitor center.

Miles and Directions

0.0 From the visitor center walk behind the restrooms and take the Razor Point Trail.

0.1 Reach a trail junction—stay on the trail for Razor Point.

0.45 Reach junction with Yucca Point and Beach Trail. Turn right to Razor Point.

0.6 Reach the Razor Point overlook. Retrace steps back to the Yucca Point/Beach Trail junction.

0.75 Arrive back at Yucca Point/Beach Trail junction; turn right.

1.0 Arrive at trail junction for Yucca Point, turn right.

1.1 Arrive at the Yucca Point overlook. Retrace steps to Beach Trail junction.

1.2 Arrive at Beach Trail junction; turn right.

1.3 Arrive at junction, turn right, and head for the beach.

1.5 Reach the junction of Broken Hill Trail and Beach Trail.

1.6 Arrive at beach; return to junction with Broken Hill Trail.

1.7 Take the right up the Broken Hill Trail.

2.5 Make a left (north) turn at the junction of the North Fork Trail.

2.8 Turn left onto North Torrey Pines Road and head back to the parking area.

3.0 Arrive at the parking area.

5 Bayside Trail

Hike along an old service road with expansive views of the Pacific Ocean and San Diego Harbor.

Distance: 2.3 miles out and back

Approximate hiking time: 1 hour

Elevation gain: 370 feet

Trail surface: Pavement and dirt road

Best season: Year-round

Other trail users: Wheelchairs, joggers

Canine compatibility: No dogs allowed

Fees and permits: Entry fee per vehicle

Maps: USGS Point Loma, CA TOPO CD 10

Contact: Cabrillo National Monument, 1800 Cabrillo Memorial Drive, San Diego 92106; (619) 557-5450; www.nps.gov/cabr

Finding the trailhead: To reach Cabrillo National Monument from the junction of Interstates 5 and 8, take I-8 west for 2 miles; exit Nimitz Boulevard/Sunset Cliffs Boulevard. Turn left onto Sunset Cliffs Boulevard and immediately turn slightly left onto Nimitz Boulevard. Drive for 1.3 miles, then turn right onto Chatsworth Boulevard. Drive south for 0.9 mile, and turn left onto Catalina Boulevard. Drive 3.0 miles on Catalina Boulevard as it becomes Highway 209/Cabrillo Memorial Drive and park.

The Hike

On September 28, 1542, Portuguese explorer Juan Rodriguez Cabrillo rounded Point Loma and became the first European to enter San Diego Bay. More than 300 years later, one of the first eight lighthouses on the Pacific Coast was installed at the crest of the 462-foot point. Both Cabrillo's

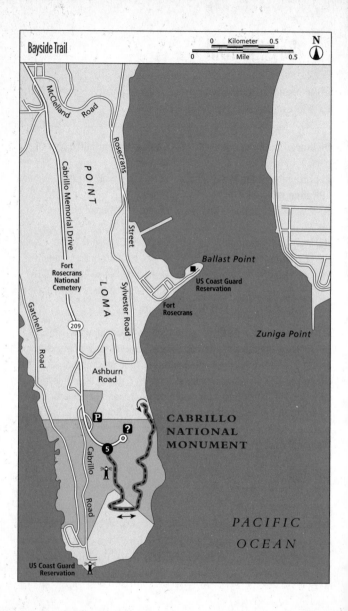

daring voyage and the Old Point Loma Lighthouse are honored by this national monument, which overlooks downtown San Diego and features 50-mile views on clear mornings. Bayside Trail takes full advantage of the views—it's often hard to resist the urge to stop and stare. The barks of sea lions and the penetrating blast of the foghorn occasionally are punctuated by the howl of fighter jets taking off from nearby North Island Air Station.

Be sure to stop at the excellent visitor center to browse through the wide selection of books on the history of the area and the region's flora and fauna.

The hike begins with a short, gentle climb from the visitor center to historic Old Point Loma Lighthouse at 0.3 mile. Fully restored, it offers an intriguing glimpse into the life of a nineteenth-century lighthouse keeper. In the days re-created here, the lighthouse was a full day's ride from its nearest neighbor.

From the lighthouse, head down the marked Bayside Trail for a few hundred yards before turning left (east) onto a steep dirt road at 0.6 mile. Pass numerous interpretive signs as you descend, as well as the remains of a World War II military defense bunker. This entire area was a vital link in the defense of San Diego during World War II, and some of the artillery gun emplacements were capable of lobbing a shell to Oceanside, nearly 40 miles up the coast. A barbed-wire fence guarding military land at 1.1 miles marks the end of the Bayside Trail. At this point, you are 90 feet above the waters of the bay.

To return, trudge back up the hill to your car along the same route, taking breaks to enjoy the views.

Miles and Directions

0.0 Head up the trail to the lighthouse at the top of the hill.

0.3 Reach the Old Point Loma Lighthouse.

0.6 Go left (east) onto the steep dirt road marked as the Bay-side Trail.

1.1 A fence marks the turnaround point. Return via the same route.

2.3 Arrive back at the parking area.

Inland Hikes

The San Diego coast is locked in "June Gloom" fog and overcast on many spring and summer days, but sunshine and warm temperatures often can be found just a few miles inland. The following hikes have this pleasant weather to recommend to them—and much more.

Characterized by undeveloped canyons, rocky hillsides, and broad mesas, the inland region covered in this guide ranges from the urban parks near downtown San Diego to the deep canyons and hill climbs 14 miles to the northeast near Poway. Sure, you'll often need to search to find a semblance of "wild" during some hikes, but their proximity to the urban sprawl makes them all the more precious.

The inland microclimate is by far the warmest in the county (except for the desert in far east county). Temperatures in the high 80s are common during summer. A midsummer, midday climb of Cowles Mountain (Hike 7) is a fool's errand. However, since many of the other hikes follow riparian streambeds choked with shade trees, even the warmer days should be bearable.

6 Tecolote Canyon

Escape the city and urbane landscape of San Diego with this quick canyon getaway.

Distance: 4 miles out and back
Approximate hiking time: 2 hours
Elevation gain: 150 feet
Trail surface: Packed dirt
Best season: Year-round, although best in the mornings and evenings during summer
Other trail users: Joggers, dogs
Canine compatibility: Leashed

dogs permitted
Fees and permits: None
Maps: USGS La Jolla, CA Topo CD 10
Contact: Tecolote Canyon Natural Park, 5180 Tecolote Road, San Diego 92110; (858) 581-9944; www.sandiego.gov/park-and-recreation/parks/teclte.shtml

---

Finding the trailhead: To reach Tecolote Canyon Natural Park from the junction of Interstates 5 and 8, take I-5 north for 0.5 mile. Exit Tecolote Road (Sea World Drive) and turn right (east) onto Tecolote Road. Continue down Tecolote Road for 0.6 mile to the Tecolote Canyon Natural Park parking lot.

The Hike

Located minutes from downtown, Tecolote Canyon Natural Park is a peaceful refuge in an urban jungle. Although the sprawl of the city is never far away, dominating the mesa tops that ring the park, the canyon bottom mostly has escaped the attention of the bulldozer and the developer.

The canyon winds for miles through dense residential communities, but only the first few miles (covered here) are easily accessible to the casual hiker. The rest of the canyon is hidden in the mystery of overgrown, steep, rocky, and muddy trails.

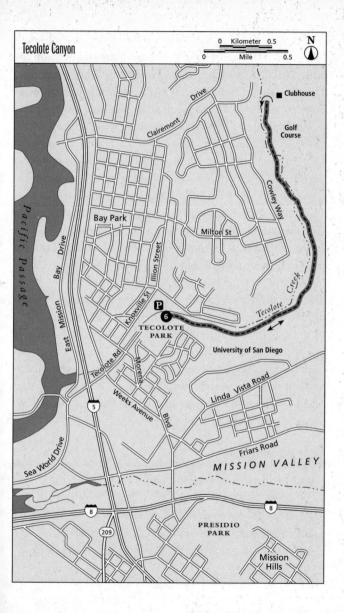

After stopping at the small visitor center at the mouth of the canyon, walk through the park gates and head up the wide trail. Before long, the surrounding houses fall away and the canyon bottom widens to reveal springtime wildflowers, a stream-supported riparian belt, and quiet groves of eucalyptus. On the bluff on your right (south) is the blue dome of the University of San Diego Catholic Church. As you continue up the canyon, you will pass beneath power lines at 1.1 miles and follow the course of the streambed as it makes a gentle left-hand turn north.

At the 1.25-mile marker, skirt the Tecolote Canyon Golf Course on the steep trail, which runs beneath wooden power poles on the south side of the canyon. Look out for stray balls from the golfers playing below the trail.

At the 1.5-mile marker, work past short but steep descents and climbs as the trail follows the contour on the south canyon wall. Just past the 1.75-mile marker, stay to the left (north) on a narrow trail that aims for the golf course clubhouse. When you reach the Tecolote Canyon Golf Course Clubhouse and the 2-mile marker, you've also reached the turnaround point. Although the trail continues on, it becomes increasingly narrow and difficult to follow. Retrace your steps to your car.

Miles and Directions

- **0.0** Leave the parking area and head east through the gates down the wide trail.
- **1.1** Pass beneath power lines as the trail veers north.
- **1.2** Skirt the golf course on left (east) side of the canyon.
- **2.0** Reach Tecolote Canyon Golf Course Clubhouse and the turn-around point.
- **4.0** Arrive back at the parking area.

7　Cowles Mountain

Hike to the highest point within San Diego city limits and gain an impressive view of the surrounding region.

Distance: 3 miles out and back

Approximate hiking time: 1.5 hours

Elevation gain: 900 feet

Trail surface: Packed dirt

Best season: Year-round, although summer days can be extremely hot, and rains in winter and spring may wash out the trail

Other trail users: Joggers, dogs

Canine compatibility: Leashed dogs permitted

Fees and permits: None

Maps: USGS La Mesa, CA TOPO CD 10

Contact: Mission Trail Regional Park, One Father Junipero Serra Trail, San Diego 92119; (619) 668-3281; http://mtrp.org

Finding the trailhead: To reach the Cowles Mountain trailhead from the junction of Interstates 5 and 8, drive east on I-8 for 8 miles and exit at College Avenue. Turn left at the fork, and follow signs for College Avenue North. Turn left onto College Avenue and drive for 1.3 miles. Turn right onto Navajo Road and drive for 2.0 miles. Turn left onto Golfcrest Drive and immediately park in the lot on the right side of the road.

The Hike

At an elevation of 1,591 feet, the summit of Cowles Mountain is the highest point in Mission Trails Regional Park and the city of San Diego. This immensely popular hike can see hundreds of trekkers a day.

There's a good reason for the crowds—the hike is a challenging workout and the views are superb, including the Cabrillo Monument, downtown San Diego, La Jolla,

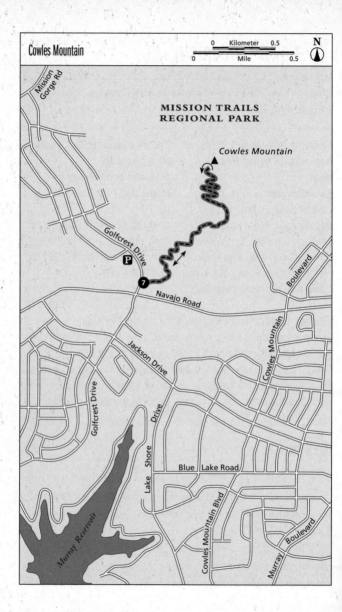

and the Pacific. On clear mornings it seems all of Southern California lies within the 360-degree summit panorama, with views of San Clemente Island (81 miles away), the San Gabriel Mountains (108 miles away), the Laguna Mountains, and Mexico.

During summer, the best time for this hike is just after dawn or near sunset. Tackling it in the middle of a summer day is a thirsty and uncomfortable prospect.

From the parking lot, join the well-worn trail and work up a series of switchbacks to the top of the first knoll, where the trail offers its first hints of the marvelous views to come. At the 0.5-mile trail marker, the trail flattens out for a short spell, then climbs the north side of the next knob. Even though you still have a ways to climb, the views should already be making the hike worthwhile.

At the trail junction at the top of the second knoll (0.7 mile), stay to the left (west) on the marked Summit Trail. From here, the going gets steep, and hikers with less stamina may want to spend a few minutes resting before continuing. Pass the 1-mile marker as you continue up.

This is the heart of the climb. Four switchbacks and the final steep pitch later, you've reached the top at 1.5 miles, and the most popular hike in San Diego County is half over.

Survey the breathtaking views from the summit, which includes two interpretive signs and a historical marker. After catching your breath, coast back down the hill, following the same trail, to your car.

Miles and Directions

0.0   Hike east up the trail from the parking area.
0.5   Reach a trail marker.

0.7 Arrive at a trail junction; continue uphill on the Summit Trail.

1.0 Reach the 1-mile marker and continue up switchbacks to the summit.

1.5 Reach the summit of Cowles Mountain. Return via the same route.

3.0 Arrive back at the parking area.

8 Oak Canyon to Grasslands Trail

Enjoy a historic dam along with the wonderful canyons and hills of Mission Trails Regional Park, one of the largest urban parks in the United States.

Distance: 2.8-mile loop
Approximate hiking time: 1.5 hours
Elevation gain: 200 feet
Trail surface: Packed dirt
Best season: Early spring
Other trail users: Joggers, dogs
Canine compatibility: Dogs permitted on leash
Fees and permits: None
Maps: USGS La Mesa, CA TOPO CD 10
Contact: Mission Trails Regional Park, One Father Junipero Serra Trail, San Diego 92119; (619) 668-3281; mtrp.org

Finding the trailhead: To reach Mission Trails Regional Park from the junction of Interstates 5 and 8, drive east on I-8 for 6.7 miles and exit onto Waring Road. After merging, drive for 1.7 miles and turn left onto Mound Avenue/Princess View Drive. Drive for 0.7 mile and turn right onto Mission Gorge Road. Drive for 1.6 miles and take a left onto Father Junipero Serra Trail. Pass the excellent visitor center on the left and continue 2 miles to the Old Mission Dam Historic Site parking lot.

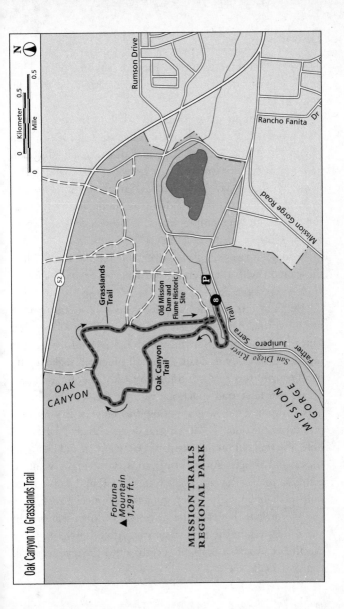

Oak Canyon to Grasslands Trail

N

0   0.5 Kilometer
0   0.5 Mile

Rumson Drive

Rancho Fanita Dr

Mission Gorge Road

52

Grasslands Trail

Old Mission Dam and Flume Historic Site

P

8

OAK CANYON

Oak Canyon Trail

Father Junipero Serra Trail

San Diego River

MISSION GORGE

MISSION TRAILS REGIONAL PARK

Fortuna Mountain
▲ 1,291 ft.

The Hike

This excellent hike features a rugged canyon, rolling hills, and begins at one of the city's most historic sites: the Old Mission Dam.

After attempts dating back to 1774 to provide a reliable source of water for crops and livestock at Mission San Diego De Alcala, located 2.5 miles downstream, this dam and flume system was finished between 1813 and 1816. Built by Kumeyaay Indian labor under the direction of Franciscan missionaries, the dam and flume are regarded as the first major irrigation engineering project on California's Pacific Coast.

Today, water still flows over the rebuilt dam, filling the canyon with the sound of flowing water and tempting anglers to drop a line.

Begin by crossing the San Diego River on an iron bridge just downstream (west) of the Old Mission Dam (0.25 mile). Once past the bridge, continue straight (north) onto the marked Oak Canyon Trail. At a trail junction, make a left-hand (north) turn and continue on Oak Canyon Trail.

At the next trail junction, veer to the left (north) on Oak Canyon Trail, which is closed to bicycles beyond this point. Just beyond a good rest spot under a shaded oak at 0.7 mile, the trail climbs into narrow Oak Canyon and becomes rocky and rough. After spring rains, you might want to pause at one of several small waterfalls, found just off the trail and hidden within deep gouges worn in the rock.

As you pass beneath the power lines, turn left (north) and briefly rejoin the main roadway. After 100 yards, leave the fire road and turn right (north) onto the marked Oak Canyon Trail.

As you near Highway 52, leave the canyon behind and make a right (east) turn onto a fire road at 1.45 miles. For a short stretch, the hike is terrifically steep, but it soon eases as you top the first of two hills. At the top of the second hill, make a left (northeast) turn onto Grasslands Trail and make a long, gradual descent to the bottom of the canyon.

Walk through the grasslands of the canyon floor, then make a right (south) turn onto the marked Old Mission Dam Trail. Take a brief detour to the Old Mission Dam viewpoint before heading west, rejoining the main trail, and returning to your car.

Miles and Directions

0.0 Head west from the parking area to the trailhead.

0.25 Cross the bridge over the San Diego River.

0.4 Turn left onto the Oak Canyon Trail.

0.6 Veer left to stay on the Oak Canyon Trail.

0.7 Turn left (west) into Oak Canyon.

1.15 Turn left onto the main roadway.

1.2 Turn right onto Oak Canyon Trail.

1.45 Go right (east) onto the steep fire road.

1.6 Stay left at the junction to join the Grasslands Trail.

2.4 Stay straight at junction to rejoin trail to parking lot.

2.45 Reach overlook of Old Mission Dam.

2.5 Turn left at junction.

2.55 Make left to rejoin trail to parking area.

2.7 Cross iron bridge over San Diego River.

2.8 Arrive at parking area.

9 Los Peñasquitos Canyon Preserve

Visit a historic adobe, hike to a splendid waterfall, and enjoy a variety of wildlife, geologic formations, and the rich cultural legacy of the preserve.

Distance: 6.3-mile loop
Approximate hiking time: 3.5 hours
Elevation gain: 300 feet
Trail surface: Packed dirt and dirt road
Best season: Winter and spring
Other trail users: Bicycles, dogs, joggers, strollers, wheelchairs

Canine Compatibility: Leashed dogs permitted
Fees and permits: None
Maps: USGS Del Mar, CA TOPO CD 10
Contact: Los Peñasquitos Canyon Preserve; (858) 484-7504; www.sandiego.gov/park-and-recreation/parks/penasq.shtml

Finding the trailhead: To reach Los Peñasquitos Canyon Preserve from the junction of Interstates 5 and 8, take I-8 east for 2.2 miles, then go north onto Highway 163 for 7.4 miles until it merges with Interstate 15. Continue north on I-15 for 3.5 miles before exiting on Mira Mesa Boulevard. Turn left and drive 0.5 mile; turn right (north) onto Black Mountain Road. The parking lot is 1.4 miles ahead on the left (west).

The Hike

Sure, it's an ambitious distance to tackle, but this 6.5-mile hike follows smooth, nearly level fire roads for most of its length, and ends at a soothing waterfall where you can soak your sore feet before heading back up the canyon. Along the way, the California live oak canopy shades great rest

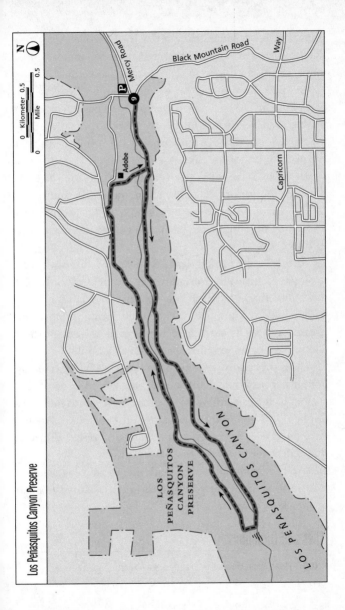

Los Peñasquitos Canyon Preserve

Black Mountain Road

Mercy Road

Way

Capricorn

Adobe

LOS PEÑASQUITOS CANYON PRESERVE

LOS PEÑASQUITOS CANYON

N

0 Kilometer 0.5

0 Mile 0.5

stops. It's no wonder that the La Jolla Native Americans lived in the area for more than 5,000 years—the oaks provided acorns, an important staple of the native diet.

In 1823 the Rancho Peñasquitos Canyon Preserve was part of the first Mexican land grant in San Diego. The oldest private residence in San Diego, the Rancho Santa Maria de los Peñasquitos Adobe, built around 1823, still stands near the parking lot for the hike.

Begin by staying left (west) at the fork in the road just north of the parking lot and heading down the south side of the canyon. A quarter-mile ahead, pass the worn white tombstone of John Eichar, a Rancho Peñasquitos cook who died in 1882.

At the 2-mile marker, leave the shade of the oaks as you stroll past a small, lush meadow on the right. Shortly past the 3-mile marker, the canyon floor narrows and is choked with boulders. During the winter and spring months, the stream cascades around these boulders in a series of short falls, providing an excellent picnic spot (3.2 miles).

Cross the narrow stream above the waterfall by carefully hopping from boulder to boulder, then head back up the canyon to the east, following the road on its north side. Stay on the north side of the canyon to visit Peñasquitos Adobe. At a junction at 3.9 miles, turn right (south) onto a dirt road that enters the shade of the oaks. This crosses the stream back to the main trail on the south side of the canyon at 4.0 miles; this is the route you walked in on. Follow the main trail back to your car.

Miles and Directions

0.0 Head west down the fire road leaving the parking area.

3.2 Reach the waterfall. Cross to the north side of the canyon.

3.3 Follow the north road to Peñasquitos Adobe.

5.5 Make a right (south) turn from the north-side canyon trail to the south.

5.6 Visit the adobe.

5.9 Make a left (east) turn onto main south-side canyon trail.

6.3 Arrive back at the parking area.

10 Blue Sky Canyon

Take a nature walk through pretty riparian, oak woodland, mixed chaparral, and coastal sage scrub environments filled with spring wildflowers and ample wildlife.

Distance: 2.5 miles out and back

Approximate hiking time: 1.5 hours

Elevation gain: 50 feet

Trail surface: Dirt road

Best season: Year-round, although during winter and early spring the trail may be very muddy

Other trail users: Joggers, dogs, horses, wheelchairs

Canine compatibility: Leashed dogs permitted

Fees and permits: None

Maps: USGS Escondido, CA TOPO CD 10

Contact: Blue Sky Ecological Reserve, 16275 Espola Road, Poway 92064; (858) 668-4781; www.blueskyreserve.com

Finding the trailhead: To reach Blue Sky Ecological Reserve from the junction of Interstates 5 and 8, take I-8 east for 2.2 miles, then exit north onto Highway 163 toward Escondido for 8.2 miles until it merges with Interstate 15. Continue north on I-15 for 11.2 miles to a right (east) turn onto Rancho Bernardo Road, which becomes Espola

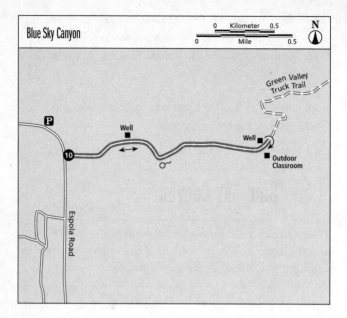

Road. The Blue Sky parking lot is 3.1 miles from the freeway on Espola Road and is on the left (north) just before a nearly 90-degree turn in the road.

The Hike

Nestled on the western slopes of Mount Woodson, the 470-acre Blue Sky Ecological Reserve holds a bounty of natural sights and sounds.

Established in October 1989 as a natural habitat, Blue Sky features several rare and threatened plant and animal species. In short succession, a hiker can find riparian, oak woodland, mixed chaparral, and coastal sage scrub environments. Each ecosystem holds its own special variety of wildlife, and the closeness of these habitats allows a great diversity of species to exist together in harmony.

This hike is especially pleasant during sunny, warm days, as the deep shade from the tree canopy keeps the creekbed relatively cool.

Begin by heading down the old dirt Green Valley Truck Trail as it winds into the canyon. After 0.25 mile, turn left (north) at the marked Oak Canyon trailhead and descend into the densely shaded canyon bottom. You've just entered the riparian belt, where the seasonal stream allows a dense canopy of trees to flourish. Pass a fence on the left and hike down the narrow trail that heads east into the heart of the canyon. Watch out for poison oak!

Rejoin the main road near an animal-tracks interpretive sign. Pass a turnoff for Lake Poway on your right (south) at 0.9 mile and continue straight (east) up the canyon.

At 1.1 miles, pass an "outdoor classroom" on the right (south). This spot includes picnic tables and a portable restroom, and is an excellent picnic spot if "class" is not in session.

At a fork in the road just past the outdoor classroom, head left (north) for a short distance, getting a view of the lay of the land as you climb onto the chaparral-covered hill. Note how the shady oaks grow only along the relatively moist canyon bottom. From here, retrace your steps to your car.

Miles and Directions

0.0 Park in the lot. Head to the south end to pick up the trail-head.

0.25 Turn left into the creekbed.

0.65 Rejoin the fire road.

0.9 Pass the Lake Poway Trail on your right (south).

1.1 Pass the outdoor classroom.

1.15 Turn left at the fork in the road.

1.25 Reach a small hill and take in the views. Return via the same route.

2.5 Arrive back at the parking area.

11 Iron Mountain

Hike to the top of a majestic mountain with sweeping views of the entire San Diego region.

Distance: 5.5 miles out and back

Approximate hiking time: 3 hours

Elevation gain: 1,000 feet

Trail surface: Dirt road, packed dirt, rock

Best season: Late fall through early spring, very hot in summer.

Other trail users: Joggers, dogs, bicycles, horses

Canine compatibility: Leashed dogs permitted

Fees and permits: None

Maps: USGS San Vicente Reservoir, CA TOPO CD 10

Contact: City of Poway, 14644 Lake Poway Road, Poway 92064; (858) 668-4770; http://www.ci.poway.ca.us

Finding the trailhead: To reach Iron Mountain from the junctions of Interstate 5 and 8, head east on Interstate 8 for 2.2 miles. Exit onto Highway 163 north (toward Escondido) and drive for 8.2 miles until Highway 163 merges with Interstate 15. Drive for 6.8 miles and exit onto Highway 56/Ted Williams Parkway. Turn right onto Ted Williams Parkway and drive for 2.5 miles. Turn right onto Twin Peaks Road and drive for 2.3 miles. Turn right onto Espola Road/S5 and drive for 0.8 mile. Turn left onto Poway Road/S4 and drive for 2.6

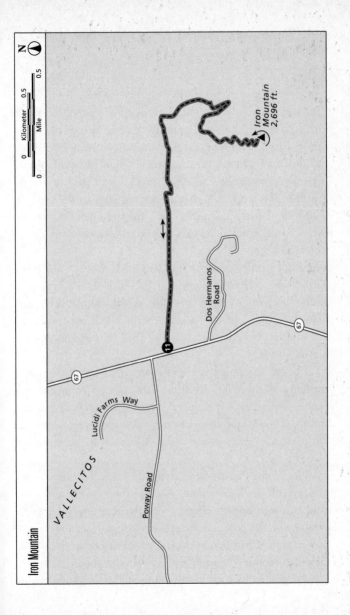

Iron Mountain

N

0   Kilometer   0.5
0   Mile   0.5

VALLECITOS

Lucidi Farms Way

Poway Road

67

11

Dos Hermanos Road

67

Iron
Mountain
2,696 ft.

miles. Turn right onto Highway 67. Parking is immediately on the opposite side of the road.

The Hike

The hike begins by walking through a shady tree-lined grove planted to line and beautify the entrance of the hike. For the first 0.5 mile, the trail to Iron Mountain follows an old fire road and travels in a straight line eastward. From here the route begins to climb quickly and the way turns into less of a road and more of a wide path to the top. At 0.75 mile the trail begins to climb the mountainside, crossing a small seasonal creek, and continues heading in an eastward direction.

At 1.25 miles into the trail, the path meets a junction. Turn right and head south on the well-signed trail and circle back around the eastern side of the summit. The trail passes a spring and climbs up a small knoll before hitting lots of little switchbacks that work their way steeply up the mountainside.

The last 0.5 mile gains elevation rather rapidly, quickly climbing 500 feet in very short succession, making the last part the toughest. The trail is steep at this point, but the views get more and more inspiring as it inches higher along the peak, so rest stops are more enjoyable as there is a lot more to see.

This is not the easiest hike in the book, but any determined soul should be able to find their way to the top with a bit of fortitude and effort. From the top, enjoy views of Poway, the San Vicente Reservoir, Barona Indian Reservation, and the coast from Carlsbad to Point Loma. Clear-day views are absolutely stunning; every prominent feature of San Diego can be seen clearly, and children and adults will both have fun pointing things out. Return via the same route, and enjoy the trip back down the mountainside.

Miles and Directions

0.0 Hike through a shady grove at the entrance of the hike and follow the old road eastward toward the summit.

0.75 The trail narrows and begins to climb the mountain.

1.25 Turn right and climb southward through a canyon.

2.25 Climb the north face of the peak up several switchbacks.

2.75 Reach the summit of Iron Mountain. Return via the same route.

5.5 Arrive back at the parking area.

Mountain Hikes

I magine a refuge of tiny streams, huge pines and oaks, archaeological sites, and incredible, awe-inspiring vistas of desert and mountain seemingly around every turn. Although it's hard to believe, such an oasis does exist, and it's less than two hours from downtown San Diego.

Forming a gentle spine through much of Southern California, the coastal mountains capture moist Pacific air and transform what would otherwise be an arid region into woodlands similar to those found in the Sierra Nevada. On the east side, the mountains end abruptly in a 4,000-foot drop. Forever locked in rain shadow, the parched desert landscape below this escarpment stretches out as far as the eye can see.

The following ten trails are located near Palomar Mountain, Cuyamaca Rancho State Park, Julian, and the town of Mount Laguna. These trails guide you through deep forests and to the tops of windswept peaks featuring 100-mile views. You'll amble along meadows and feel the smooth granite of a basin where Native American women ground acorns hundreds of years ago. Quite simply, this is the best hiking San Diego County has to offer.

The mountains of San Diego could be characterized as a gentle wilderness. However, hikers must be prepared for quick changes in temperature—especially in the winter and spring months (November through April). In a single day, the weather can shift from burning sun to bone-chilling showers or snow. Be prepared for both extremes; carry a windbreaker and other clothing items to protect you from rain and/or sudden, dramatic temperature changes.

One word of caution can't be overlooked. There are dangerous critters that you may encounter in this region, like mountain lions, bobcats, coyotes, and rattlesnakes. Mountain lions are a continuing concern in the region, and it's wise to stop by the park headquarters or a USDA Forest Service ranger station to acquaint yourself with tips for avoiding trouble with these predators. Many parks post signs that will help you identify and avoid potential hazards. Carefully read these notices—it's advice worth following.

12 Doane Valley

Wander through an idyllic and peaceful forested glen filled with wildflowers and wildlife.

Distance: 2.25-mile loop
Approximate hiking time: 1.5 hours
Elevation gain: 100 feet
Trail surface: Packed dirt
Best season: Year-round
Other trail users: None
Canine compatibility: No dogs allowed

Fees and permits: Parking/day-use fee per vehicle
Maps: USGS Boucher Hill, CA TOPO CD 10
Contact: Palomar State Park, 19952 State Park Drive, Palomar Mountain 92060; (760) 742-3462; www.parks.ca.gov/?page_id=637

Finding the trailhead: To reach Doane Valley for the intersection of Interstates 5 and 8, head east on Interstate 8 for 2.2 miles. Exit onto Highway 163 north (toward Escondido) and drive for 8.2 miles. Merge onto Interstate 15 and drive for 34.1 miles to Highway 76/Pala Road. Exit and turn right onto Highway 76/Pala Road and drive for 10.5 miles. Turn left onto Adams Drive and drive 0.5 mile. Turn left onto Gomez Trail and drive for 7.6 miles. Stay straight at the junction with Palomar Divide Firebreak Truck Trail. Continue for 3.3 miles. Stay straight at Doane Valley Road. Continue for 1.8 miles and park in the lot on the left.

The Hike

Doane Valley is a peaceful and wonderfully wooded parcel of land in Palomar Mountain State Park. Both idyllic and pastoral, this hike contains the best of all the region has to offer. From the parking area, circumnavigate Doane Pond,

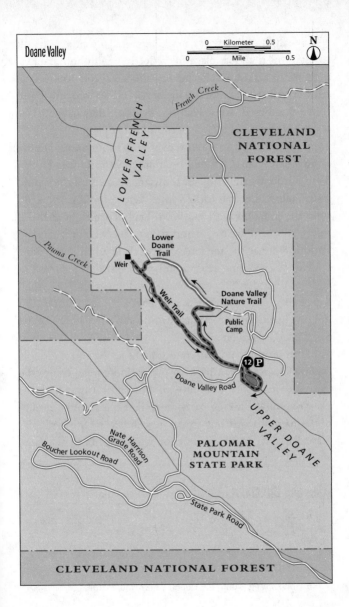

a heavenly body of water nestled among the pine and oak forest. This is a great place for reflection and photography.

Cross back through the parking area and follow the nature trail as it borders Doane Creek. A brochure and thirty numbered stops describe the plant life, habitat, and some of the natural history of the area. People of all ages will enjoy the informative interpretive walk. From the end of the nature trail, take a left and continue on the Lower Doane Trail bordering the same meadowlands passed on the nature trail. Follow this trail for 0.5 mile, before turning left again onto the junction with the Weir Trail. Turn right at the T intersection and follow a short path to the weir and gauging station. Here at the meeting of French, Pauma, and Doane Creeks, the gauging station and weir were constructed in 1920 to consider the possibility of building a dam. No such dam exists, due to the inconsistency of constant water, but the precipitation here eventually flows to the Pacific via the San Luis Rey River.

Turn around and continue straight at the junction, following Doane Creek back to the parking area. Truly, the ease and magnificent beauty of this short trip will leave everyone in the hiking party amazed at the absolute beauty of the natural world and in the peaceful wonder of Palomar State Park. Keep an eye out for wildlife of both the large and small variety.

Miles and Directions

0.0 From the parking lot head south to Doane Pond and circle the pond.

0.3 Walk across the parking lot and cross Doane Valley Road and walk up the Weir Trail.

0.5 Make a right onto the Doane Valley Nature Trail.

0.8 Turn left onto the Lower Doane Trail.

1.2 Turn left to meet the junction with the Weir Trail.

1.3 Turn right and head to the weir. Retrace steps to the junction.

1.4 Stay straight on the Weir Trail and continue back to the parking area.

2.25 Arrive back in the parking area.

13 Volcan Mountain

Hike to the top of a graceful mountain preserve overlooking the Julian Valley.

Distance: 5 miles out and back
Approximate hiking time: 2.5 hours
Elevation gain: 1,200 feet
Trail surface: Packed dirt road
Best season: Year-round
Other trail users: None
Canine compatibility: No dogs allowed

Fees and permits: None
Maps: USGS Julian, CA TOPO CD 10
Contact: Volcan Mountain Preserve, 1209 Farmer Road, Julian 92036; (760) 765-2300; www.volcanmt.org

Finding the trailhead: To reach Volcan Mountain from the junction of Interstates 5 and 8, take Interstate 8 east for 37.4 miles. Take the Highway 79/Japatul Road exit toward Julian. Turn left onto Highway 79 and drive for 2.8 miles. Turn left to stay on Highway 79 and drive for 20.2 miles. Turn right onto Highway 78 and drive for 2.1 miles. Turn left onto Wynola Road and drive for 0.8 mile. Turn right onto Farmer/Volcan Road. Park along the road.

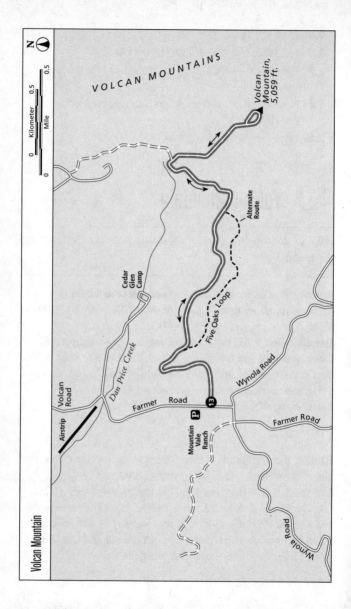

Volcan Mountain

The Hike

Volcan Mountain is magnificent, windswept, and set above the historic mining town of Julian, its apple orchards, and the sprawling desert of Anza-Borrego to the east. From on high, expansive views in the park span across Southern California and provide one of the major highlights of the hike.

Climbing to the top of Volcan Mountain showcases the fascinating piece of land north of Julian that is gradually gaining in size due to conservation efforts and attempts to acquire surrounding lands in order to maintain and preserve the natural habitat of this beautiful mountain area.

The hike begins along the main entrance into the preserve and follows an old dirt service road all the way to the top. At 0.2 mile, the preserve entrance is marked by an awesome sculpture that resembles something from another world. Turn left and stay on the wide trail as it meanders through mixed pine and oak forest and open grassland. The trail climbs almost the entire route, but the grade is rather gentle and the ever-expanding views of the Cuyamacas, the desert, and the Pacific become a reward in their own right. The road junctions twice with the Five Oaks Loop, which can be taken on the return by those who wish to add a bit of variety to the hike.

As the trail nears the summit, it becomes less shaded. Stay on the road and cross through the gate at 1.6 miles to continue on to the summit. At the top, the roadway loops around, and a bench and various relics await those ready to take a respite.

Follow the same route back down the mountain, or turn off onto the Five Oaks Trail for some adventure. This trail adds virtually no mileage to the hike and covers the same distance, elevation, and terrain of the old road.

Miles and Directions

0.0 Park on the roadway and follow the old dirt road as it climbs up the spine of Volcan Mountain.

0.2 Make a left and head north on the road through the gate next to the sculptured monument.

0.6 Stay straight on the road at the junction with the Five Oaks Loop; note the stone steps on the right.

1.3 Stay straight on the road with the second junction with the Five Oaks Loop.

1.6 Go through the gate and continue on the road to the top.

1.8 Take the right fork at Simmons Flat and head for the summit of Volcan Mountain.

2.5 Arrive at the summit. Return via the same route.

3.3 Arrive at intersection with Five Oaks Loop.

4.0 Arrive at second intersection with Five Oaks Loop.

5.0 Arrive back at the preserve entrance.

14 Stonewall Mine/Lake Cuyamaca Hike

Visit a historic mine and stroll through tall pines beside a quiet lake.

Distance: 2.6-mile loop
Approximate hiking time: 1.5 hours
Elevation gain: 100 feet
Trail surface: Packed dirt and dirt road
Best season: Year-round
Other trail users: None
Canine compatibility: No dogs allowed

Fees and permits: Parking/day-use fee per vehicle
Maps: USGS Cuyamaca Peak, CA TOPO CD 10
Contact: Cuyamaca Rancho State Park, 13652 Highway 79, Julian 92036; (760) 765-3020; www.parks.ca.gov/default .asp?page_id=667

Finding the trailhead: To reach the Stonewall Mine/Lake Cuyamaca Hike from the junction of Interstates 5 and 8, take I-8 east for 37.4 miles to Highway 79/Japatul Road and turn left (north). Head north for 10.7 miles to a parking lot on the right (north) side of the highway, just south of Lake Cuyamaca. The trail leads north toward the lake from the parking area.

The Hike

It's just after dawn. In the middle distance, mist gently rises from a mirror–smooth lake. The sun is still a half hour from cresting the eastern hills; deep shadow locks the forested lake shore in calm. Nearby, a twig cracks and five mule deer cross the trail, their white tails swishing in the windless

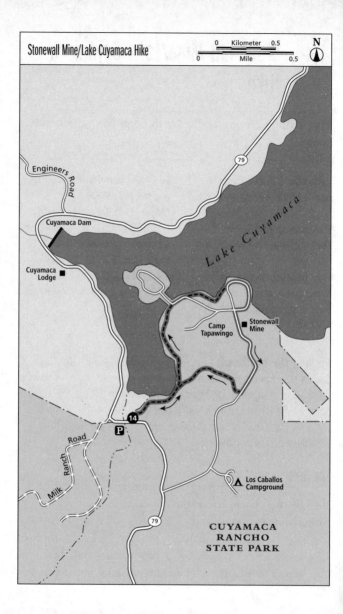

Stonewall Mine/Lake Cuyamaca Hike

0   Kilometer   0.5
0   Mile   0.5

N

Engineers Road

Cuyamaca Dam

Cuyamaca Lodge

Lake Cuyamaca

79

Camp Tapawingo

Stonewall Mine

14

P

Milk Ranch Road

Los Caballos Campground

79

CUYAMACA RANCHO STATE PARK

morning. You smile and start to walk. For 2 more miles, similar sights await you.

Besides offering incredible hiking, this trail also passes the Stonewall Mine, site of the largest and most lucrative gold mine in Southern California. At the height of the gold rush, from 1886 to 1891, the Stonewall Mine employed 200 people and yielded more than 100,000 ounces of gold. The mine was closed and its main shaft sealed in 1892. A small museum and interpretive center are now located nearby.

From the parking lot, head north on the unnamed trail, crossing a shallow seasonal stream before contouring along the bottom of a hill to a trail junction at 0.3 mile. Turn left (north) at the junction.

Cross an earthen causeway that bisects wetlands. At the end of the causeway, squeeze past a gap in the fence and turn right (west) along the edge of the Cuyamaca reservoir (0.7 mile). A short way farther up the shoreline, take another left (north) turn at a trail junction as you amble alongside the water.

As you contour around to the north side of the small hill on your right, leave the shore momentarily before making a left (north) turn onto a trail marked Los Caballos Horse Camp at 0.9 mile. Head down the hill to broad views of the meadow northeast of the lake, bearing east, then southeast. After a few hundred yards, make a right (west) turn onto a trail marked Stonewall Mine Site.

Climb a hill to the mine at 1.2 miles, visiting each of the interesting displays. Then, make a left (southeast) turn onto a paved road. Walk down the road (ignoring a gated side road to the left/east) for a few hundred yards to a right (west) turn onto an unnamed dirt trail that heads uphill. Work over the hill before making a right (northwest) turn at an unnamed trail junction. Rejoin the trail you came in on and retrace your steps to your car.

Miles and Directions

0.0 Leave the parking area north on the unmarked trail.

0.3 At the trail junction, stay left, angling toward the lake.

0.5 Cross the causeway over the wetlands.

0.7 At the trail junction, stay right along the lake.

0.9 At the trail junction, turn left onto the trail to Los Caballos Horse Camp.

1.2 At the trail junction, make a right (west) turn to the Stonewall Mine site.

1.5 Visit the old site and the small cabin that serves as a museum.

1.9 Make a right turn onto an unnamed dirt trail.

2.0 Stay straight on the trail.

2.25 Turn left to return to the trail to the parking area.

2.6 Arrive back at the parking area.

15 Stonewall Peak

Hike up a steady and fairly easy grade to a tremendous overview of Cuyamaca Rancho State Park where over one hundred summits in Southern California can be identified.

Distance: 4 miles out and back

Approximate hiking time: 2 hours

Elevation gain: 860 feet

Trail surface: Packed dirt and rock

Best season: Spring or fall

Other trail users: None

Canine compatibility: No dogs allowed

Fees and permits: Parking/day-use fee per vehicle

Maps: USGS Cuyamaca Peak, CA TOPO CD 10

Contact: Cuyamaca Rancho State Park, 13652 Highway 79, Julian 92036; (760) 765-3020; www.parks.ca.gov/default .asp?page_id=667

Finding the trailhead: To reach Stonewall Peak from the junction of Interstates 5 and 8, take I-8 east for 37.4 miles to Highway 79/Japatul Road and turn left (north). Drive for 2.8 miles. Turn left again to stay on Highway 79 and drive for 9.3 miles and turn left (west) into Paso Picacho Campground. Use the parking lot just to the right (north) of the campground entrance.

The Hike

Standing as quiet sentinel over much of southern Cuyamaca Rancho State Park, the exposed summit of Stonewall Peak offers an irresistible call to hikers of all ages. It's all uphill to the summit, but the grade never exceeds 6 percent, and the vistas are extraordinary. Once shady and forested, this hike was devastated in the Cedar Fire of 2003, but has deservedly remained one of the most popular hikes in the park.

Stonewall Peak

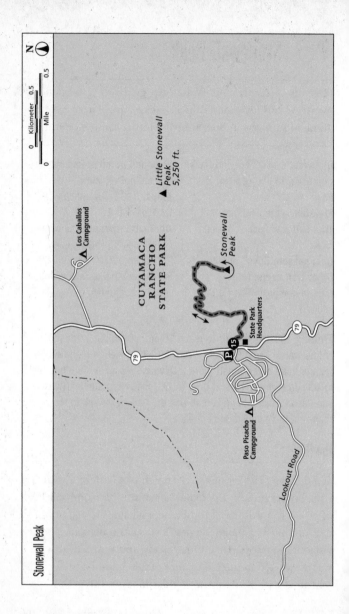

While the panorama from the top is simply stunning, the views aren't limited to the summit. As the trail cuts back and forth across the flanks of the mountain, past numerous switchbacks, the vistas alternate between the Sweetwater River valley in the south to Lake Cuyamaca in the north.

From the Paso Picacho parking lot, cross Highway 79 to the Stonewall Peak Trailhead. Pass a large boulder to excellent trailside vistas of the remaining forests and meadows to the south, then traverse across to the northwest side of the peak.

Once on the northern flanks of the peak, the trail climbs through five switchbacks to a large granite slab on the northwest side of the peak. Take a break and catch your breath as an expansive view of Lake Cuyamaca stretches out below. Continue up past fourteen more switchbacks to a marked trail junction for Los Caballos Horse Camp at 1.8 miles. Turn right (west) at the junction.

The trail levels before steeply climbing to the exposed granite of the summit. A helpful handrail near the top will keep you on track. If you're lucky, you may see rock climbers scaling the south face of the peak. Watch your step and keep an eye on your children while on the summit. Although clearly defined with a metal guardrail and easy to follow, the summit trail is exposed and thrilling—a perfect climax to an excellent hike.

To return, retrace your steps to your car, enjoying the wonderful views as you descend.

Miles and Directions

0.0 Cross Highway 79 from the parking area to reach the trailhead.

0.25 Begin heading north along the trail.

1.8   Reach the trail junction for Los Caballos Horse Camp. Take the right fork to the top.

2.0   Arrive on the summit of Stonewall Peak. Return via the same route.

4.0   Arrive back in the parking area.

16   Pioneer Mail Trail

Walk to Kwaaymii Point, an incredible vantage point in the Laguna Mountains, and take in the expanse of Anza-Borrego Desert State Park overlooking a 4,000-foot escarpment.

Distance: 1.5 miles out and back
Approximate hiking time: 45 minutes
Elevation gain: 200 feet
Trail surface: Packed dirt road and partial pavement
Best season: Spring
Other trail users: Dogs, bicycles
Canine compatibility: Dogs permitted

Fees and permits: None
Maps: USGS Monument Peak, CA TOPO CD 10
Contact: Cleveland National Forest Descanso Ranger District, 3348 Alpine Boulevard, Alpine 91901; (619) 445-6235; www.fs.fed.us/r5/cleveland or Laguna Mountain Recreation Area, (619) 473-8547; www.lmva.org

Finding the trailhead: To reach Pioneer Mail Trail from the junction of Interstates 5 and 8, take I-8 east for 44.5 miles to Sunrise Highway (California S1) and turn left (north). Follow Sunrise Highway for 15.7 miles to milepost 29, where a right turn at the Pioneer Mail Picnic Area and trailhead will deposit you at a parking lot. The trail begins on the northern side of the parking lot.

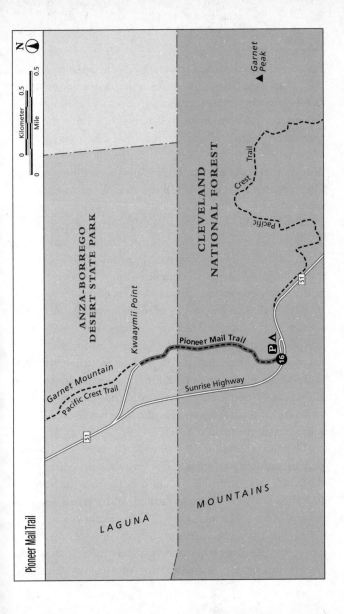

Pioneer Mail Trail

The Hike

Part of the appeal of the Laguna Mountains is the huge eastern escarpment that drops away to the desert floor—4,000 feet below the forested mountain slopes. The transition is abrupt: forest one moment, 100-mile desert views the next. Incredibly rugged canyons connect the desert and mountains, which served as migration routes for the Kwaaymii Indians as they headed to higher elevations during spring. On summer days, you can feel the heat of the desert as the wind whistles up the canyon walls.

This hike slowly reveals one of these canyons as it works along an old section of the Sunrise Highway, which was hewn into the side of Garnet Mountain. Taking neither much time nor energy to complete, this hike provides one of the best views in the Laguna Mountains.

The hike starts by passing an interpretive sign on an old section of the Sunrise Highway. As this sign makes clear, this portion of the old highway was once an airy and thrilling ride. The highway also served as an important mail route to the mountain communities to the northwest. The Cleveland National Forest is allowing this portion of road to revert to its natural state, but the hike is still smooth and suitable even for small children.

Head up the hill as the view of Cottonwood Canyon unfolds; the canyon quickly falls away to the desert floor. Resist the urge to trundle rocks into the canyon below—this disturbs wildlife, hastens erosion, and presents a serious danger in the off chance there are hikers below you.

As the road begins to cut into the hillside, the views down into the canyon become vast, and the full scope of the canyon can be appreciated. At the turnaround (0.6 mile), the trail reaches Kwaaymii Point, where the hot summer wind whistles up from the desert floor 4,000 feet below.

Once you've had your fill of gawking at the views, cruise back down the hill to your car. The PCT continues northward to Canada from the point through the lovely Anza-Borrego Desert State Park. Those wishing to continue the stroll may do so for as long as the views continue to inspire.

Miles and Directions

0.0 Leave the parking area to the north along the old roadway.

0.75 Reach Kwaaymii Point. Return via the same route.

1.5 Arrive back at the parking lot.

17 Garnet Peak

Hike to the summit of Garnet Peak, showcasing one of the best views in all of Southern California—a great destination for watching sunrises.

Distance: 2.5 miles out and back
Approximate hiking time: 1.5 hours
Elevation gain: 560 feet
Trail surface: Packed dirt and dirt road
Best season: Early mornings during the summer
Other trail users: Dogs, horses
Canine compatibility: Dogs permitted
Fees and permits: Adventure Pass required for parking
Maps: USGS Monument Peak
Contact: Cleveland National Forest Descanso Ranger District, 3348 Alpine Boulevard, Alpine 91901; (619) 445-6235; www .fs.fed.us/r5/cleveland or Laguna Mountain Recreation Area; (619) 473-8547; www.lmva.org

Finding the trailhead: To reach Garnet Peak from the junction of Interstates 5 and 8, take I-8 east for 44.5 miles to Sunrise Highway (California S1) and turn left (north). Follow Sunrise Highway for 14.3 miles to a small parking area on the right (east) side of the highway, just before milepost 28. The marked Garnet Peak trailhead is just to the east.

The Hike

The summit of Garnet Peak will send shivers of joy down your spine and, if the weather is clear, might offer the most spectacular views in San Diego County. Reach the trailhead before dawn for a sublime experience on the summit. Don't forget a jacket on this hike—the summit can be cold.

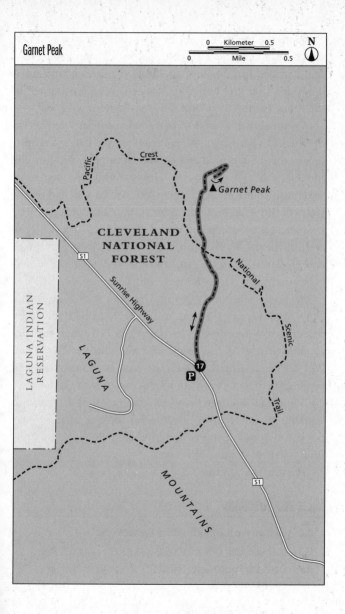

Garnet Peak

0 Kilometer 0.5
0 Mile 0.5

N

Pacific Crest

Garnet Peak

CLEVELAND
NATIONAL
FOREST

S1

Sunrise Highway

LAGUNA INDIAN RESERVATION

LAGUNA

National

Scenic

17
P

Trail

MOUNTAINS

S1

From the trailhead, join the marked trail to Garnet Peak, which wanders down through some remaining pine and fire-damaged forest before climbing to a split in the trail at 0.3 mile. Take the left (west) fork. This region burned in the Pines Fire of 2002, and most of the trees were lost.

Continue past a stand of burnt oaks on relatively flat trail to where the Pacific Crest Trail intersects the trail at 0.6 mile. Ignore the PCT turnoff and continue straight (north) up the route as it begins to climb in earnest. While the best vistas are ahead, your toil up the steep trail will be softened by the views of the rolling mountainside to the northwest.

Head up the steep and rocky trail, which works up the western flanks of the mountain. With each step through the chaparral, as you gain altitude and near the desert escarpment, the views become more impressive.

As you make your way up the final 0.25 mile to the exposed and rocky summit, you're likely to be buffeted by nearly continuous desert winds that moan through the surrounding rocks. If you've planned your hike well, the sun will just be clearing the eastern horizon as you near the top, turning the desert below into an ocean of pink sand.

The wind-whipped, exposed summit is spectacular, with a seemingly sheer drop of thousands of feet to the desert floor. Obviously, parents should keep a close eye on children when attempting this hike.

Return as you came.

Miles and Directions

0.0 Start on the trailhead north to Garnet Peak.

0.3 At a side trail, stay left (north) and pass a large oak tree.

0.6 Cross the Pacific Crest Trail (PCT) and head straight up through chaparral.

1.25 Arrive at the summit of Garnet Peak. Return via the same route.

2.5 Arrive back at the trailhead.

18 Oasis Spring

Hike through an austere and arid desert canyon to a lush and gentle spring.

Distance: 2 miles out and back
Approximate hiking time: 1 hour
Elevation gain: 330 feet
Trail surface: Packed dirt
Best season: Spring or summer
Other trail users: Dogs, horses
Canine compatibility: Dogs permitted
Fees and permits: Adventure Pass required for parking

Maps: USGS Monument Peak, CA TOPO CD 10
Contact: Cleveland National Forest Descanso Ranger District, 3348 Alpine Boulevard, Alpine 91901; (619) 445-6235; www .fs.fed.us/r5/cleveland or Laguna Mountain Recreation Area, (619) 473-8547; www .lmva.org

Finding the trailhead: To reach Oasis Spring from the junction of Interstates 5 and 8, take I-8 east for 44.5 miles to Sunrise Highway (California S1) and turn left (north). Follow Sunrise Highway for 12.9 miles to a small parking lot on the right (east) side of the highway at milepost 26.5. The trailhead is just before the turnout.

The Hike

If, after completing the hike up Garnet Peak or out to the Cottonwood Canyon viewpoint, you find yourself

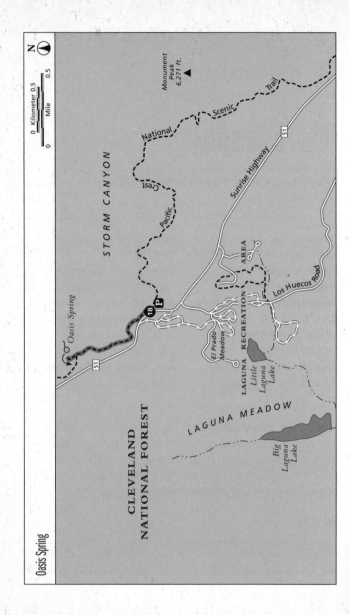

Oasis Spring

wondering what life in one of the steep canyons leading to the desert is like, this is the hike for you. Oasis Spring is a patch of oak trees and a trickle of water in the otherwise rugged and dry Storm Canyon. Even when the desert far below is locked in shimmering heat waves, this spot offers cool shade—perfect for a picnic or a nap.

This hike also uses a portion of the 2,550-mile Pacific Crest Trail, which runs from the Mexican border to Canada. Walking along the PCT, you can feel its almost magnetic pull and hear its promise of adventure. Imagine walking for four months through wilderness and still not reaching trail's end! Truly an odyssey of Homeric proportions.

From the parking lot, head down the hill to the Pacific Crest Trail and turn left (north). Continue on the PCT as it climbs a small knoll and passes a relatively new fire road at 0.3 mile. Ignore this fire road and continue down the hill on the PCT. Keep a sharp eye out for animal tracks in the soft dirt of the trail; this is a major thoroughfare for animals of all types that call this area home.

The Pacific Crest Trail merges onto a dirt road at 0.5 mile and then quickly leaves it. Where the routes diverge, leave the PCT and continue right (north) down the canyon on the dirt road. As the steep road works its way along the wall of Storm Canyon to near its northern crook, the exposed chaparral-covered hillside gives way to oak trees and shade. The shade deepens; listen for the telltale tinkling of Oasis Spring. Numerous picnic sites are nearby.

After thoroughly enjoying the cool peace around the spring, tighten your shoelaces and sweat your way up the road and trails as you retrace your steps to your car.

Miles and Directions

0.0 Head south from the parking area and access the Pacific Crest Trail (PCT) heading north.

0.3 At the first dirt road, continue straight (west) on the PCT.

0.5 Continue straight (north) on the dirt road after the PCT merges with it.

1.0 Arrive at Oasis Spring. Return via the same route.

2.0 Arrive back at the parking area.

19 Lightning Ridge

Hike to a stunning overlook of Laguna Meadow and then stroll along its green northern boundary.

Distance: 1.5-mile loop
Approximate hiking time: 1 hour
Elevation gain: 900 feet
Trail surface: Packed dirt
Best season: Spring
Other trail users: Dogs
Canine compatibility: Dogs permitted
Fees and permits: Adventure Pass required for parking

Maps: USGS Monument Peak, CA TOPO CD 10
Contact: Cleveland National Forest Descanso Ranger District, 3348 Alpine Boulevard, Alpine 91901; (619) 445-6235; www .fs.fed.us/r5/cleveland or Laguna Mountain Recreation Area, (619) 473-8547; www .lmva.org

Finding the trailhead: To reach Lightning Ridge/Horse Heaven Meadow from the junction of Interstates 5 and 8, take I-8 east for 44.5 miles to Sunrise Highway (California S1) and turn left (north). Follow Sunrise Highway for 12.6 miles. Turn left at Laguna Meadow

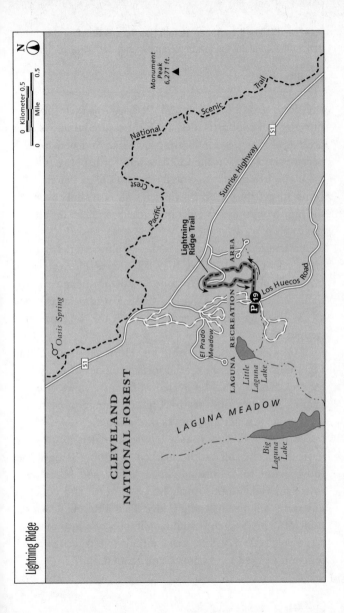

Lightning Ridge

Road, and follow it as it merges with Los Huecos Road for 0.6 mile. Park in the lot along the road entering Laguna Campground.

The Hike

Meadows have a special appeal. Perhaps it is their promises of water and cool grass. Perhaps it is because meadows offer great opportunities for spotting wildlife. And perhaps it is because a meadow is the ultimate spot for napping.

If you like meadows, you'll enjoy this hike. After a short climb to get the blood flowing, it's all downhill to one of the numerous meadows that make the San Diego mountains such a treat.

From the parking lot near the amphitheater, head east and walk 0.15 mile along the trail toward Horse Heaven Group Campground. A stone cenotaph designates the trailhead for Lightning Ridge. Cross a seasonal creek bed and walk alongside the meadowland. At the fork, continue straight.

Turn left at the junction for Horse Heaven. Climb Lightning Ridge Trail up the forested slopes of the hill to the top, where you'll be treated to fantastic views of upper Laguna Meadow and nearby Laguna Campground to the southwest. A water tank marks the summit.

From the viewpoint at 0.7 mile, turn left (south) and head down the hill on the marked Lightning Ridge Trail (now a fire road) through huge Jeffrey and sugar pines to a hard right (south) turn. Make the turn and continue down the hill on Lightning Ridge Trail, cruising down the switchbacking trail and catching glimpses of a lush meadow to your left. At 1.1 mile, make a right (west) turn at a trail junction marked for Laguna Campground.

Miles and Directions

0.0 Park near the amphitheater near Laguna Campground. The trail begins by the stone monument.

0.3 Make a left turn onto the marked Lightning Ridge Trail.

0.7 Arrive at a viewpoint. From the hilltop, turn left (south) down the fire road.

1.1 At the junction by the meadow, turn right (west) to Laguna Campground.

1.5 Arrive back at the parking area.

20 Kwaaymii Trail

Enjoy a short interpretative trail that highlights the culture and remaining relics of the Native Americans who once inhabited these mountains.

Distance: 0.5-mile loop

Approximate hiking time: 30 minutes

Elevation gain: 320 feet

Trail surface: Packed dirt

Best season: Year-round

Other trail users: Dogs

Canine compatibility: Dogs permitted

Fees and permits: Adventure Pass required for parking

Maps: USGS Mount Laguna, CA TOPO CD 10

Contact: Cleveland National Forest Descanso Ranger District, 3348 Alpine Boulevard, Alpine 91901; (619) 445-6235; www .fs.fed.us/r5/cleveland or Laguna Mountain Recreation Area, (619) 473-8547; www .lmva.org

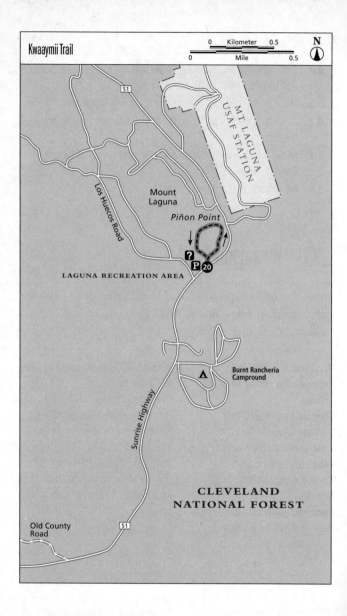

Finding the trailhead: To reach Kwaaymii Trail from the junction of Interstates 5 and 8, take I-8 east for 44.5 miles to Sunrise Highway (California S1) and turn left (north). Follow Sunrise Highway 9.9 miles to the town of Mount Laguna at milepost 23.5. Turn left onto Los Huecos Road and park at the visitor information center just to the north of the Mount Laguna store.

The Hike

Like the Paso Nature Trail in Cuyamaca Rancho State Park, the self-guided Kwaaymii Trail offers excellent insight into the natural history of the region. This trail primarily highlights the Kwaaymii Indians, who inhabited this region hundreds of years ago.

These Native Americans passed the winter in the low, warm desert valley to the east, then climbed the steep canyons looking for respite from the harsh summer sun. Evidence of their passage is found throughout San Diego's mountains; that evidence can be seen along this short trail in the form of *morteros* (deep holes) and *metates* (shallow depressions) where Kwaaymii women would grind one of the staples of the tribal diet—acorns from the numerous black oaks found nearby. Before traveling the short loop to the top of the hill, make sure to pick up the interpretive flyer at the visitor information center.

Join the Indian Trail at a marked sign just to the west of the visitor center. As you climb the short hill, pause at each of the numbered waypoints, which correspond to the information found on the flyer. On the summit of the hill, take time to feel how the rock has been smoothed to a glasslike surface in the numerous morteros and metates. With a commanding view of the surrounding area, it's no wonder the Kwaaymiis chose this site for one of their summer homes.

The cool mountain breezes no doubt were a welcome relief from the searing temperatures of the desert below. A large pinyon pine, which is somewhat rare at this elevation, also grows on the summit, and views of the forested hills stretch around you.

Head down the hill, pausing at the numbered waypoints found along the well-marked trail, back to the visitor information center and your car.

Miles and Directions

0.0 The trail begins behind the visitor center.

0.05 Head right at the fork to follow the interpretive loop.

0.25 Reach viewpoint.

0.5 Continue the loop to the visitor center.

21 Wooded Hill Nature Trail

Wander through pine trees to a small summit with dazzling overlooks of the Pacific Ocean and an expansive 200-mile panoramic view.

Distance: 1.5-mile loop
Approximate hiking time: 1 hour
Elevation gain: 300 feet
Trail surface: Packed dirt
Best season: Year-round
Other trail users: Dogs
Canine compatibility: Dogs permitted
Fees and permits: Adventure Pass required for parking

Maps: USGS Mount Laguna, CA TOPO CD 10
Contact: Cleveland National Forest Descanso Ranger District, 3348 Alpine Boulevard, Alpine 91901; (619) 445-6235; www .fs.fed.us/r5/cleveland or Laguna Mountain Recreation Area, (619) 473-8547; www .lmva.org

Finding the trailhead: To reach Wooded Hills Nature Trail from the junction of Interstates 5 and 8, take I-8 east for 44.5 miles to Sunrise Highway (California S1) and turn left (north). Follow Sunrise Highway for 8.2 miles to a left (north) turn marked with a Wooded Hills Campground sign. The parking lot is 300 yards down this road, on the left (west) side of the road.

The Hike

If you've completed some of the other hikes found in the mountains of San Diego County, you've seen views north across the desert, east to the Salton Sea, and south from Stonewall Peak, but you haven't seen any vistas west toward San Diego and the Pacific. Walk the easy-to-follow Wooded Hill Nature Trail when the air is especially clear

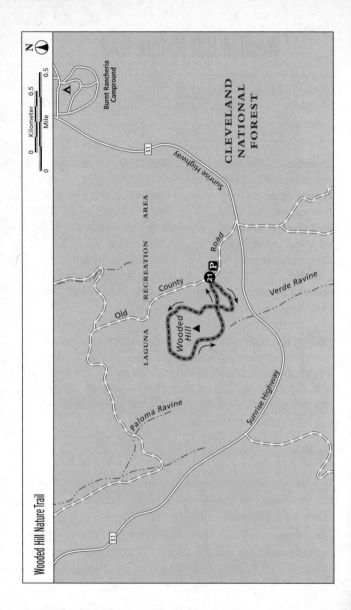

Wooded Hill Nature Trail

and you'll see a 200-mile panorama that reaches from the deserts to the east, far into Mexico to the south, and out west to San Diego and the blue ocean.

Even if you're not fortunate enough to find a clear day on which to hike, you'll still find the Wooded Hill Nature Trail a pleasant journey, meandering up through pines and small boulders to its 6,220-foot summit.

From the parking lot, pass the signed trailhead and begin to work up the southern slopes of the hill. The trail is narrow but smooth for most of its length, making this an excellent hike for children.

After climbing for a little over 0.25 mile, make a left (west) turn at a trail junction marked LONG LOOP. Continue the gentle climb to the top of the hill. As you traverse the top, you'll come to a viewpoint where on a clear spring day you'll be treated to vistas that stretch away in all directions.

From the summit, head north through a boulder garden before heading down the northwest slopes of hill, passing a water tank on your left. The trail continues back around to the east side of the hill, where, at 1.3 miles, it intersects the Long Loop turnoff you took earlier. From this point, make a left (east) turn onto a trail marked TO TRAILHEAD and descend back to your car.

Miles and Directions

0.0   Head west on the southernmost trail from the parking area.

0.25 Make a left at the junction that says LONG LOOP.

0.6   Reach viewpoint.

1.3   Make a left at junction that says TO TRAILHEAD.

1.5   Arrive back at parking area.

Desert Hikes

Anza–Borrego Desert State Park is an enormous desert wonderland filled with adventure. It is the second-largest state park in the nation and the largest in California. Washes, wildflowers, mountains, wildlife, palm canyons, incredible views, and historical artifacts are just some of the many great things about the park. Hundreds of miles of trails and roads line the park, and it is a great place to explore from top to bottom.

Three hikes are highlighted in the park, and they take into consideration some of the best variety that Anza-Borrego has to offer. Certainly they are but a small sampling, and visitors can only do justice to this magnificent park by spending more time in the region.

Hiking in the desert brings with it certain dangers. Flash floods, extreme heat and cold, dehydration, and snakebite are more common in these arid climes. Please use more caution when hiking in canyons, especially during winter or spring, and be mindful of the time, the view on the trail, and your surroundings. Pack in extra food, extra water, and layered clothing in case of temperature extremes.

Enjoy the land, but respect its power.

22 Ghost Mountain

Visit a surreal homestead atop the lonely and expansive ridgeline of Ghost Mountain.

Distance: 1 mile out and back
Approximate hiking time: 1 hour
Elevation gain: 400 feet
Trail surface: Packed dirt, sand, and rock
Best season: Late fall through early spring
Other trail users: Horses
Canine compatibility: No dogs allowed
Fees and permits: None
Maps: USGS Earthquake Valley, CA TOPO CD 10
Contact: Anza-Borrego Desert State Park, P.O. Box 299, Borrego Springs, CA 92004; (760) 767-5311; www.parks.ca.gov/default.asp?page_id=638

Finding the trailhead: To reach Ghost Mountain from the junction of Interstates 5 and 8, take Interstate 8 east for 37.4 miles. Turn left onto Highway 79/Japatul Valley Road and drive for 2.8 miles. Turn left to stay on Highway 79 and drive for 20.2 miles. Turn right onto Highway 78 and drive for 11.3 miles. Make a slight right at Great Southern Overland Stage Road/S2 and drive for 5.8 miles. Make a slight left at the dirt road (at mile 22.9) signed for GHOST MOUNTAIN, PORTREROS, AND PICTOGRAPHS. Drive for 2.8 miles and make a left at the parking road signed for GHOST MOUNTAIN.

The Hike

Ghost Mountain is sure to leave an indelible mark on all who make the trek to its most famous artifact. Yaquitepec, as it was named by its founders, is the remains of the adobe homestead of Marshal and Tanya South, who lived on this spot for fourteen years. Here they raised a family apart from

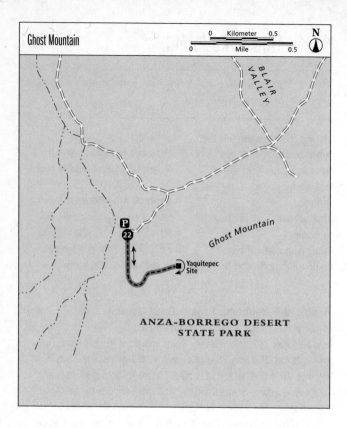

civilization in a deliberate attempt to bring their children up in a decent world away from the greed and distraction of modern society.

Marshal was an author and artist who documented his family's life on the mountain for *Desert Magazine*. Their austere and rugged existence on the mountain is both inspiring and incredible. Many remnants of their everyday life still remain, and Ghost Mountain seems an aptly fitting title for such a place. The experiment at Yaquitepec did not last as the Souths split in an acrimonious divorce, and Tanya with her children never spoke about their lives or what happened. Marshal died shortly after leaving the mountain.

Now the mountain and its environs are encompassed within the boundary of Anza–Borrego Desert State Park. From the parking area, walk south up the mountainside. The trail is easy to follow and within 0.5 mile the ruins will be discernible. The way is a bit rocky, but not at all technical. Be sure to keep ankles steady on the trail. An old box-spring mattress, some walls, and a large cistern attest to the impossible task living must have been in this harsh ecosystem.

Those with extra energy can make the trek to the top of the mountain, adding 2.5 miles to the total distance, and those who want to just thoroughly enjoy the archaeological significance of this place can take lots of time and return whenever.

Miles and Directions

0.0 Leave the parking area to the south following the clear trail up the mountain.

0.5 Reach Yaquitepec. Return via the same route.

1.0 Arrive back in the parking area.

23 Borrego Palm Canyon

Hike to a secluded palm grove and peaceful waterfall in California's largest state park.

Distance: 2.4 miles out and back

Approximate hiking time: 1.5 hours

Elevation gain: 500 feet

Trail surface: Packed sand, sand and dirt

Best season: Late fall through early spring

Other trail users: Horses

Canine compatibility: No dogs allowed

Fees and permits: None

Maps: USGS Borrego Palm Canyon, CA TOPO CD 10

Contact: Anza-Borrego Desert State Park, P.O. Box 299, Borrego Springs, CA 92004; (760) 767-5311; www.parks.ca.gov/default.asp?page_id=638

Finding the trailhead: To reach Borrego Palm Canyon from the junction of Interstates 5 and 8, head east on I-8 for 37.4 miles. Turn left onto Highway 79/Japatul Road and drive for 2.8 miles. Turn left to stay on Highway 79 and continue for 20.2 miles. Turn right onto Highway 78 and drive for 18.3 miles. Turn left onto S3/Yaqui Pass Road and drive for 6.9 miles. Turn left onto Borrego Springs Road/S3 and drive for 5.3 miles. At the roundabout, head west on Palm Canyon Drive for 2.0 miles. Turn right and follow Anza-Borrego Desert State Park for 1.8 miles to the parking lot.

The Hike

Borrego Palm Canyon is a beautiful remnant of what once was. Hundreds of California fan palms historically graced the thirsty wash that meanders its way into Borrego Springs. In 2004 a flash flood wiped out most of the trees that grew

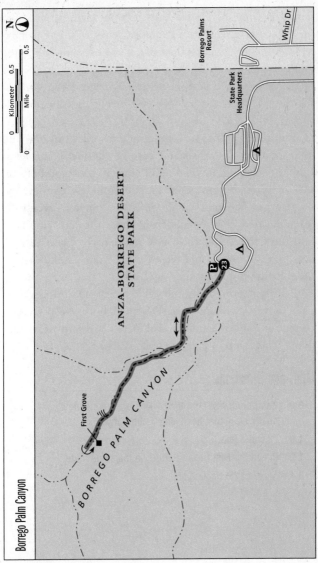

Borrego Palm Canyon

here, but some of the hardiest specimens still survive, and the beauty that remains is exquisite. Most of the remaining trees sit higher up along the canyon's floodplain, due to the rapid rush of water that channeled past and swept away most of the trees in the bottom of the drainage. Even without the history, the palm grove is still lovely and deserving of a visit.

From the parking area, head up the well-worn trail into the canyon as it narrows and becomes distinctive of desert washes in the region. The trail follows the canyon bottom, and interpretive signs point out common desert shrubs and vegetation. The trail climbs into the canyon, eventually reaching a small waterfall. From there the trail continues into the setting now known as First Grove. The trail ends here, and visitors should return via the same route or take the short loop spur on the way back.

Just after spring rains, the wildflowers and shrubbery can come alive in vibrant hues. Desert bighorn sheep are also common along the trail, and it is not unheard of to spot them. This is a trail that everyone will enjoy.

Miles and Directions

0.0 Head northwest from the parking area along the clearly marked trail that heads into Palm Canyon.

1.0 Pass the falls.

1.2 Reach the First Grove. Return via the same route.

2.4 Arrive at the parking area.

24 Calcite Mine

Visit an old mine, view bizarre desert landscapes, and explore fantastic slot canyons.

Distance: 3.5 miles out and back

Approximate hiking time: 2 hours

Elevation gain: 650 feet

Trail surface: Sand, dirt, and rock

Best season: Late fall through early spring, do not enter slot canyons during rain or times of runoff

Other trail users: Horses, four-wheel-drive vehicles

Canine compatibility: No dogs allowed

Fees and permits: None

Maps: USGS Seventeen Palms, CA TOPO CD 10

Contact: Anza-Borrego Desert State Park, P.O. Box 299, Borrego Springs, CA 92004; (760) 767-5311; www.parks.ca.gov/default.asp?page_id=638

Finding the trailhead: To reach Calcite Mine from the junction of Interstate 5 and 8, head east on I-8 for 37.4 miles. Turn left onto Highway 79/Japatul Valley Road and drive for 2.8 miles. Turn left to stay on Highway 79 and continue for 20.2 miles. Turn right on Highway 78 and drive for 18.3 miles. Turn left at S3/Yaqui Pass Road and drive for 6.9 miles. Turn left at Borrego Springs Road/S3 and drive for 5.3 miles. At the roundabout drive east on Palm Canyon Drive/S22 toward the Salton Sea, and drive for 19.4 miles. Park off the roadway on the northern side of the road.

The Hike

Anza-Borrego is a great state park for four-wheel-drive vehicles. It is also a great place to hike and enjoy desert scenery in near solitude. This hike takes place on a dirt road

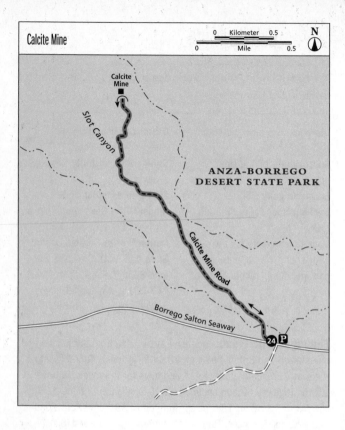

open to four-wheel-drive vehicles and heads for a secluded mine in the heart of the desert. While there is no guarantee that there will be no one else on the trail, it is fairly certain that the traffic will be light, but one option to keep in mind is that those with high-clearance off-road vehicles can drive to the mine and its remnants. The road is not in the best shape, and only experienced off-roaders should attempt it.

However, one of the best things about driving in is that more time can be focused on exploring the slot canyons which line the topography of this section of the park. Wind and water have steadily eroded the rock and created amazing caverns and ravines that dot the region. Walking in has its positives, too; it is a lot easier to spot the best canyons on foot, and an unlimited amount of time can be spent exploring them.

From the Borrego Salton Seaway (S22), walk north on Calcite Mine Road. The road is easy to follow, and it will not be difficult to stay on the trail. At 1.3 miles the road crosses a deep wash. Here is where the adventure can split: Heading north up canyon along the wash will enter the surreal world of slot canyons; staying on the roadway will take the hiker to a wonderful mine. Depending on the amount of time and water, enthusiastic hikers can try both. Those armed with a GPS can trek through the canyon and find the mine after exiting.

The mine is interesting and well worth a trip, and finding the way out is simple: Just head back down the road. The intrepid, however, might have more interesting adventures in mind. Should hiking parties choose to explore canyons, make certain to advise others in advance of those plans. Hiking in slot canyons can be dangerous.

Miles and Directions

0.0 Leave Palm Canyon Drive and hike north on the Calcite Mine Road.

1.3 Reach an awesome slot canyon on the left. Explore it or continue to the mine.

1.75 Reach Calcite Mine. Return via the same route.

3.5 Arrive back at parking area.

Day Hiker Checklist

Use this list or create your own, based on the nature of your hike and personal needs.

Clothing
- ☐ hat
- ☐ fleece jacket
- ☐ rain gear
- ☐ swimsuit
- ☐ extra socks

Footwear
- ☐ comfortable hiking boots
- ☐ water shoes or sandals

Food and Drink
- ☐ trail mix
- ☐ snacks
- ☐ water

Photography
- ☐ camera
- ☐ film
- ☐ accessories
- ☐ dry bag

Navigation
- ☐ maps
- ☐ compass
- ☐ GPS unit

Miscellaneous

- ❑ pedometer
- ❑ binoculars
- ❑ watch
- ❑ daypack
- ❑ sunglasses
- ❑ sunscreen
- ❑ insect repellent
- ❑ first-aid kit
- ❑ toilet paper
- ❑ small trowel or shovel
- ❑ extra plastic bags to pack out trash
- ❑ flashlight
- ❑ batteries
- ❑ knife/multipurpose tool
- ❑ matches in waterproof container and fire starter
- ❑ this hiking guide

About the Updater

Allen Riedel is a photographer, journalist, author, and teacher. He lives with his wife, Monique, and children, Michael, Sierra, and Makaila. He writes an outdoor column for the *Press Enterprise* and has authored several hiking guides, including *100 Classic Hikes in Southern California, Best Hikes with Dogs in Southern California, Best Easy Day Hikes Riverside,* and *Best Easy Day Hikes San Bernardino*. He lives in Riverside, California.